Songs for the Journey

Songs
for the Journey

THE PSALMS IN LIFE AND LITURGY

Brian Pickett

DARTON·LONGMAN + TODD

First published in 2002 by
Darton, Longman and Todd Ltd
1 Spencer Court
140–142 Wandsworth High Street
London sw18 4JJ

ISBN 0–232–52384–3

A catalogue record for this book is available from the British Library.

Designed by Sandie Boccacci
Phototypeset in 12¼/13pt Perpetua by Intype London Ltd
Printed and bound in Great Britain by Page Bros, Norwich, Norfolk

For Elizabeth

Contents

Preface

I have loved the psalms since I was a choirboy. While the New Testament often seemed to seek an idealized world, more in the mind than in the flesh, the psalms were a world full of raw beauty and true to life. They sang of wind and sea, woods and fields; with them you could smell spices and taste honey. They were not afraid to pray in anger against bullying enemies or give voice to doubt and despair. If they were the word of God, I felt God knew what it was like to be human.

The psalms were written to be sung by people together, the people of God. When our own joy and pain are shared, we are changed by our fellow pilgrims and come to know the God who is incomparably greater than our needs of the moment.

In worship we see how these songs shape our society as well as our personal faith. They come from a people who struggled with God as they journeyed through the wilderness of harsh landscape and doubting heart, a people who caught a glimpse of God in the pillar of fire, the hastily eaten Passover meal, and the tent of meeting which travelled with them. The God of the psalms is the God who awaits us on the horizon. They lead us, in company with others, across the unknown threshold of new relationships in baptism and marriage. They help us journey in hope through the inhospitable terrain of suffering and bereavement. They take us away from our preoccupation with what I can get out of God to a fuller vision of ourselves in the world. Together with others, we find ourselves loved, cherished and transformed in our communion with God. Through the psalms we see creation in a new light and find ourselves helping to build a community of love and trust.

I have drawn upon the wealth of the Church's many traditions and explored insights (which Christians usually ignore) from rabbinic Judaism, past and present, insights which occasionally throw unexpected light on the life of Jesus, for whom the psalms were a formative influence.

We are not given the option of standing still in our lives. We travel on through good and bad, well or not so well. Praying the psalms offers no simple directions but it keeps us in touch with reality, a reality experienced and transfigured with the love of God.

> Your statutes have become songs for me,
> wherever I make my home on my travels.
>
> *Psalm 119.54*

BRIAN PICKETT

ONE

On the Edge of Glory

Crossing the threshold

Crossing the threshold of a church can be a daunting experience.
People who devotedly tend graves would still never enter the
church itself. Wedding guests will wait outside until the last
moment before braving unfamiliar territory, fortified by a quick
cigarette. It is even difficult for regular churchgoers who have
been bereaved or who have suffered some other trauma which
makes them wary of meeting people, including God. The Psalmist
records the encouragement of going in company to worship:

> I was glad when they said to me,
> 'Let us go to the house of the Lord.'
>
> *Psalm 122*

Churches try to overcome these inhibitions by posting friendly
bands of sidespeople at the door to welcome the congregation.
They design comfortable foyers to break down the barriers and
make worship accessible. Worshippers may even walk into a café
area, complete with kitchen and bar-stools.

Yet we are not just coming into someone's lounge. These 'in-
between' places and times of transition, like the church door,
need to be recognized as places of both danger and opportunity,
for this is 'where the real discernment takes place, where we
have to listen to ourselves and look at life to discover which move
or which change will take us that bit closer to our own truth and
its living'. Tibetan Buddhists, for example, interpret the place
between death and rebirth as the great 'gap', full of danger and

temptation, yet 'in the transition and uncertainty of change lies the opportunity for awakening'.[1] For those who come across the Church's threshold to celebrate rites of birth, marriage and death, there is, therefore, a proper, if subconscious, feeling of wariness.

The danger of opening that door to a new world is well illustrated in the Welsh myth of Branwen and his veterans who take refuge from defeat in an island palace. Its stately hall has two doors which open and a third, 'the door we must not open'. For 80 years they blissfully ignore it until one of them daringly opens it to see what will happen. 'And when he looked, they had such an awareness of every loss they had ever experienced, and of every friend and companion they had lost, and every ill that had happened to them, as if it had just befallen them.'[2] The opening of the door and the subsequent journey to bury their dead leader offered them an opportunity to resolve their ambivalent refugee status and cross an emotional threshold, releasing the past and entering the reality of the present. Arnold van Gennep, the anthropologist, showed how societies use such 'ritualistic traversing of territory', often symbolized by a rite at the threshold, to integrate a stranger or a prospective bridegroom or reincorporate into the community those who have returned from a precarious experience beyond the bounds of normal life, such as war, puberty, childbirth or bereavement.[3] The ritual brings the whole community to accept and support the person. This was the role fulfilled by the Hebrew priest when he declared clean those who had recovered from various illnesses, a social and religious function recognized by Jesus himself (Luke 5.14 cf. Lev. 14).

Some of these insights were developed further in the work of Victor Turner, who examined how movements like that of Francis of Assisi nurtured this communal solidarity by compelling the friars to 'inhabit the fringes and interstices of the social structure' and keeping them 'in a permanently liminal state'.[4] Pilgrimages where rich and poor would share the insecurity of the journey and their various needs for forgiveness or blessing created similar bonds across social classes. Christians inherited this pilgrim ideal from the experience of Jews, who are commanded to remember their origins in the insecurity of a homeless ancestor, 'the wandering Aramaean' (Deut. 26.5). Some of this shared history of living in between slavery and freedom, which was to be repeated so often for the Jews, is ritualized in the Passover, when people are enabled to cross the boundary of hope from being no-people to God's people.

The barrier of sin

Jewish liturgy also helped the congregation to cross another boundary: the gap between what God requires of us and the life we actually live. Worshippers came face to face with the demands of the Law and crossed the threshold from sin to a renewed commitment to God.

Perhaps the most dramatic encounter of this kind awaited the pilgrims who had wound their way up to the Temple mount and stood before the gate, seeking entry with words from a ritual preserved in Psalms 15 and 24, which still introduce some services on the Sabbath:

> Lord, who may live in Your tent,
> who may dwell on the mountain of Your holiness?
>
> *Psalm 15* (FPJW)

The priestly guardian of the gate replies, setting before the pilgrims the lifestyle that true worship entails:

> Whoever follows integrity
> and does what is right
> and speaks the truth in their heart.

Worshippers could not be expected to be perfect but they should examine whether they were really committed to God's ways. The company of pilgrims would answer that they were approaching God in the right spirit.

> This is a generation that searches for Him,
> those who seek Your presence are the family of Jacob.

In processional liturgies when the Ark was borne up to the Temple, symbolizing the presence of the Lord, the commitment

of the worshippers to the Law they carry gives them courage to
demand of the gatekeepers:

> Gates, lift up your heads!
> Be raised, you everlasting doors!
> let the king of glory enter!

In a ritual exchange which heightens the sense of occasion and
expectation, the gatekeepers encourage the people to identify
and acclaim the one who comes:

> Who is this king of glory?

And the procession shouts out their faith:

> The Lord of all creation,
> He is the king of glory!

Psalm 24 (FPJW)

What it means to seek God is spelt out in a Jewish Midrash
which visualizes someone approaching the gates of heaven with
the request, 'Open to me the gates of righteousness.' They in
turn are asked, 'What was your work?' If they reply, 'I fed the
hungry . . . I gave drink to the thirsty', they will be told, 'This is
the gate of the Lord. Enter into it, you that fed the hungry . . .
gave drink to the thirsty.'⁵ The welcome we receive at God's door
is bound up with the welcome that we offer those in need at our
own door, for the threshold of God and that of our own hearts
cannot be separated.

Medieval churches vividly taught people the moral consequences of worship, for they were made to enter the house of
God beneath frescoes or reliefs of the Last Judgment over the
west door or the chancel arch. The Reformers offered a similar,
if wordier, challenge by confronting the congregation with the
Ten Commandments on either side of the altar. But the challenge
to be done with sin as we cross the threshold of the church had
been part of its earliest traditions, as we can see in Psalm 141 at
Orthodox Vespers. Apart from its obvious suitability for the time
of day, John Chrysostom explains that it was chosen 'as some
saving treatment and medicine for the purification of sins, so
that, through this spiritual song, at the coming of evening we may

purify ourselves of everything which might have defiled us during
the day, whether we were in the city centre, at home, or elsewhere'.[6] The imagery of the door was dramatized by the clergy
entering the sanctuary as this invitatory psalm was sung.

> Let my prayer be set forth in your sight as the incense:
>   and the lifting up of my hands as the evening sacrifice.
> Hear me, Lord.
> Keep guard, Lord, over my mouth:
>   and place a door around my lips.
> Do not turn away my heart to words of evil:
>   or to excuses for excusing my sin.

In the daily worship of the Iona Community the proclamation
of righteousness in God's realm is followed through with other
psalm texts that urge us to seek justice and reconciliation as we
come to God.

> The world belongs to God,
>   *The earth and all its people.*
> How good it is, how wonderful
>   *To live together in unity.*
> Love and faith come together,
>   *Justice and peace join hands.*
> If Christ's disciples keep silent
>   *These stones would shout aloud.*
> Open our lips, O God,
>   *And our mouths shall proclaim your praise.*
>
> *Psalms 24, 133, 85, 51*

The responsive setting helps the congregation to own this
vision of love for God and for our neighbour.

The gate of heaven

Coming into God's house we enter not just a different place with
other values but a different world. The ikons on the royal doors
of an Orthodox sanctuary reveal the saints of heaven: they are
gates of mystery, welcoming worshippers to God's world. And
the cry in the Orthodox Liturgy '*The doors! The doors!*' indicates

that only the baptized have the spiritual vision to see God revealed in the Eucharist. We can only travel so far in worship before commitment is needed to open the doors of the kingdom. Then we are taken into the realm of angels, archangels and all the company of heaven. Already in Judaism, this eternal dimension of praise had come to be expressed by the repeated response of the congregation joining their praises with the chorus of heaven.

> The Lord reigns, let the peoples tremble;
> He is enthroned on the cherubim, let the earth quake.
> The Lord is great in Zion,
> He is exalted above all the peoples.
> They praise Your name as great and awesome. He is holy!
>
> Exalt the Lord our God,
>   and bow down at His footstool; He is holy!
>
> Exalt the Lord our God,
>   and bow down at His holy mountain;
>   for the Lord our God is holy.
>   *Psalm 99.1–3, 5–9* (ADPB)

In Isaiah's vision this triple antiphon is echoed by the seraphim in heaven who respond to each other as they sing:

> Holy, holy, holy is the Lord of hosts:
>   the whole earth is full of God's glory.
>   *Isaiah 6.3*

The Temple rites hovered between the earthly representation and the heavenly reality. This was emphasized by its orientation which enabled the morning sun to shine through the doors into the haze of incense before the Holy of Holies, catching the glint of the golden cherubim enfolding the Ark.[7]

The Christian Church also adopted the Sanctus to give voice to our communion with heaven. The liturgy, as Tertullian suggested, is a preparation and a rehearsal for the fullness of life to come, so that, as the hosts incessantly chant 'Holy, holy, holy', 'we also, if we have proved worthy, are candidates to join the angels and already we are learning by heart that heavenly address

to God and the service of the glory that is to be'.[8] For many
believers (perhaps more than for agnostics) such rumours of
angels are an embarrassment, except as a Christmas decoration.
Yet angels persist in Scripture, poetry, art and the world of the
imagination. The painter Cecil Collins, for example, depicts both
landscape and the approaches to the city with these spiritual
beings, asserting that angels are something we have to wrestle
with for they draw us, against all reason, into another conscious-
ness of the world.[9] Significantly, they appear in the liturgy at the
Sanctus, the very point when the physical and spiritual are
brought together at the consecration of bread and wine.

Other traditions emphasize how this communion with heaven
strengthens us in our journey of holy living. The Malabar Liturgy
of south India concludes the Eucharist with this ancient hymn
attributed to Ephrem:

> Let the eyes which have beheld your great mercy
>   also behold the blessed hope which is from you.
> Dispose the tongues which have cried 'Holy'
>   for the speaking of truth.[10]

The joy and expectation of that Sanctus hymn overflows in
Charles Wesley's hymnody into the search for holiness in our
own pilgrimage, where God is already inaugurating the kingdom
and fulfilling our Lord's Prayer.

> Happy the souls to Jesus join'd,
>   And saved by grace alone;
> Walking in all Thy ways we find
>   Our heaven on earth begun.
>
> The Church triumphant in Thy love,
>   Their mighty joys we know;
> They sing the Lamb in hymns above,
>   And we in hymns below.
>
> Thee in Thy glorious realm they praise,
>   And bow before Thy throne;
> We in the kingdom of Thy grace,
>   The kingdoms are but one.

The holy to the holiest leads,
From hence our spirits rise,
And he that in Thy statutes treads
Shall meet Thee in the skies.

Here the threshold of the church is no longer a barrier but, like Jacob's ladder, a way through into a kingdom of God, where heaven and earth cannot be divided. A Xhosa call to worship from South Africa boldly rings out the invitation to eternity:

Sabelani! Sabelani! Niyabizwa ezul wini!
Answer! Answer! You are called to heaven!

The one who comes

The gates of mystery reveal the kingdom of God because they are also, as Jews call them, gates of mercy, showing the God who longs to be seen and known in love as well as glory among us. For Christians it is above all at the Eucharist that we receive God into our midst. In the Early Church this welcome was anticipated at the offering of the bread and wine, when it seems that the congregation sang '*Lift up your heads, O you gates, and let the King of glory enter*'. A sixth-century patriarch berates those 'who have taught the people to sing a certain psalmic chant when the ministers are about to bring up to the altar the bread of oblation and the recently mixed chalice: in this hymn, which they consider suitable to the action being performed, the people say that they bear in the King of glory' (a phrase unique to Psalm 24).[11] The practice survives in the Armenian rite and inspired the great Cherubic Hymn sung at the procession of bread and wine in Orthodox services. The version used in the Lenten Liturgy of the Presanctified Gifts, attributed to the seventh century, comes closest to the language of the psalm.

Now the hosts of heaven invisibly worship with us,
For see, here enters the King of glory.

Remarkably, the only other liturgy in which the song of the Psalmist accompanied the offertory was in the Presbyterian Church of Scotland, whose communion service retained a rubric until 1994 that the psalm 'Ye gates lift up your heads' should be sung as the bread and wine are brought into church and laid on the holy table.

The welcome for Christ is carried into the Eucharistic Prayer itself with the anthem which follows the Sanctus, 'Blessed is he who comes in the name of the Lord'. Bryan Spinks suggests that this addition (not found in Judaism) may have been introduced as a proper anthem for Easter. A fourth-century Cappadocian preacher comments on the same text in Matthew 21.9 in his Easter homilies, associating it with the newly baptized who can now sing the hymn of praise which they had never heard before.[12] Here Jewish tradition may have been influential for Psalm 118, from which the Benedictus comes, is one of the psalms sung at the Passover meal. Our expectation of the one who has led a pilgrim people triumphantly through the waters of death is fulfilled in communion together. In the Orthodox Liturgy the meal is heralded by priest and deacon appearing at the royal doors, elevating the Body and Blood of Christ before us with the words:

> With reverence for God, faith and love, come near . . .
> Blessed is the one who is coming in the name of the Lord.
> The Lord is God and has appeared to us.
>
> *Psalm 118.26–7*

We not only meet God but we share in the mystery of God through the communal experience of a meal. There is nothing esoteric about the food or the guests: they are as ordinary as a carpenter's supper, yet everything and everyone here is revealed in a new light.

For as we welcome the one who comes, we are welcomed. We open the door of church and heart to Christ who seeks to come and sup with us, and Christ opens for us a door to eternity which none may shut. Christ is indeed the gate for the sheep; in his coming the Advent antiphon greets him as the 'Key of David' and Celts sing of his birth as a 'Door of happiness' while his communion with us is acclaimed in one Urdu lyric as '*the way and the door for the poor*'.[13] The gospel of the passion and resurrection itself shows us one who will not leave us behind like orphans but who takes us on the journey across the threshold of death. The

victor of the cross is about to enter paradise as king, but not
before he has brought the penitent thief with him, and at his
death tombs carved into the rock face are split open. The
theological iconography of Christ descending to save the departed appears explicitly in the New Testament and his victory
is portrayed as a public procession of triumph (Luke 23.42–3;
Matt. 27.50–2; 1 Pet. 3.19; 4.6; Col. 2.15).

The path to paradise

Our participation in Christ's Easter journey transfigures every
threshold that we have to cross, including the frontier of life and
death. Early Christian tradition drew upon the imagery of Psalm
118 and its association with the Eucharist to affirm that those
who shared his supper were also led by him in a procession of
triumph through the gates of death. By the eighth century Psalm
118 was sung during the funeral procession from the church to
the grave, accompanied by lights and incense.[14] Sometimes it is
sung as the grave is asperged with water and incensed. The later
medieval period overlaid the service with penitential psalmody,
but even then Christian funerals could resound to the joy of the
response:

> Open to me the gates of righteousness:
>   and I will go into them.
> I will give thanks to the Lord:
>   this is the gate of the Lord, the righteous shall enter
>   into it.
>
> *Psalm 118.19–20*

In the psalm the victory procession of the Hebrew king leads to
the decoration of the altar with garlands of green branches and
fruits. This has been interpreted as a primitive rite to awaken
and transfer a holy force to the altar as a source of blessing. The
Christian parallel would be the carpeting of graves with ever-
green leaves, as witnessed already in fourth-century Spain by
Prudentius in his funeral hymn, where the grave is covered with
leaves and flowers and people pray that Christ will guide the

departed to the open path which leads to the sacred wood of paradise.[15]

The Orthodox burial service still retains a remnant of this bold imagery. For a priest the whole of Psalm 24 is chanted but at all funerals the body is laid to rest and the priest scatters dust upon it in the sign of the cross with the words:

> The Lord's is the earth and its fullness:
> the world and all who dwell in it.

The earth of the grave is claimed by its Creator and Sovereign in whose name it is to take and cherish the departed until resurrection. The dramatic dialogue of the psalm demanding that the gates of death lift up their heads for the King of glory is illustrated in ikons of the resurrection. The risen Christ descends to raise the dead from their dark captivity, shattering the doors of hell and scattering broken hinges, bolts and keys. For Christians brought up in the synagogue, this psalm had an immediate resonance with the resurrection because it was the psalm set for the first day after the Sabbath, that is Easter Day. Already in Rabbinic Judaism there were eschatological interpretations which linked it with Isaiah 22.6 as a commentary on the general resurrection of the dead at the end of time.[16]

As early as the second century the Apocalypse of St Peter adds verses from Psalm 24 in response to a vision the disciples experience, revealing Christ's ascension and the reward of the righteous. This vision was read in some Palestinian churches on Good Friday, presumably after the passion, and so it seems to have become part of the Easter Vigil. A fourth-century sermon for that occasion certainly makes the most of what had become a familiar text in the liturgy:

> Who is this King of glory who does in hell what has never happened in hell before? Who is this who leads forth from there those who have been in everlasting sleep? Who is this King of glory? The Lord powerful and mighty, the Lord mighty and strong, unconquerable in the struggle![17]

The singing of Psalm 24 at the Easter Vigil may also have inspired the composition of the canticle '*Te Deum*' with its celebration of

Christ as the King of glory opening the kingdom of heaven to all believers. Some scholars have concluded that it was originally a eucharistic preface written in the fourth century for the Easter Vigil, echoing the imagery of the psalm earlier in the liturgy. Traces of this canticle survive in the Eucharistic Prayer of St Basil in the Egyptian rite.[18] In the Coptic Church the psalm remains as part of the Vigil, marking a transition between the Lord's answer to the plight of the poor ('I will rise up' Ps. 12.5) and the triumph of the ascension ('God has gone up' Ps. 47.5). Evidence suggests, however, that it had been more widely used in the ninth and tenth centuries in Celtic lands after the Good Friday Liturgy and in Italy following the lighting of the New Fire.[19]

By the medieval period, this psalmody had become part of a veritable drama. After the Good Friday Liturgy, the crucifix and host were buried in a place representing the tomb and, usually before Matins on Easter Day, they were raised and brought to the altar sometimes with verses from Psalm 24. The Easter Office of the Nuns of Barking in Essex (c. 1370) offers us the best evidence to hand. Here the abbess led her convent to the chapel of St Mary Magdalene where they were shut in. The priest and ministers come with cross and banner, crying out 'Lift up your gates' as they pound the door with the cross to represent Christ breaking the doors of hell. The same dramatic presentation is found in William Langland's description of the harrowing of hell and the medieval miracle plays.[20]

We see, then, that in the Easter Liturgy worshippers were moved, often literally in procession, across the threshold of death with their crucified and risen Lord opening the gates of paradise; an occasion on which they must have reflected on their own journey through death to life. They carried this hope into their funerals, singing Psalm 118 in the faith that at death Christ opens for us the gate to life. Psalm 24 was also sung on the way to the grave in medieval Milan, and its survival at Orthodox funerals suggests that it was once more fully used.[21] Our need is certainly no less than that of our forebears and these psalms assure us that God has opened the door for us at the very time when it seems irrevocably shut. As we walk the way of the Easter Christ with the songs on our lips that sustained him, we discover that his journey is also ours. The music together with the text carries us with it but we should not forget the power of drama in ritual and story to open our eyes to the realm of the kingdom. We need a liturgy week by week which draws all ages into the drama of the Christ event and helps us identify with our guide for the journey.

Our going out and coming in

The glory of the risen Christ sheds light on all our journies, not only that at our ending We know that coming home and leaving home are often moments of potential joy or sorrow, excitement, anger, even depression. And we, in the West, sometimes have no idea how to express our confused emotions and reactions in a safe way because we have lost the rituals which many religions have. In Judaism word and action are combined in the touching of the Mezuzah scroll attached to the doorpost, the kissing of the finger which has touched it and the repetition of Psalm 121 first used by the priest to bless Temple pilgrims. Irish Christians would celebrate their homecoming with the same words from Psalm 118 which took their departed home to God. In such ways we become aware that every homecoming, every leave-taking, has the potential to carry a significance beyond opening or closing the door behind us.

The strength of the psalms is that their music binds us together in the solidarity of singing which can travel anywhere and stay with us in our memory. They are the ideal medium for a pilgrim people, as the Jews found when the Temple was destroyed. Many of its cultic practices could not be transferred and there was considerable debate about whether they should be continued. A similar story could be told of the Protestant Reformation. But music and musicians transcend such arguments. Music crosses the barriers of race and religious practice. It guides us through loss and change, because it is tied to no place and travels with no baggage except the human voice and heart. Yet it can evoke for us in any time or place the security of traditional rhythm and melody and carry a strength of faith beyond any present constraints. So with the psalms we are always at home with God and with the people of God praying with us at every crossroads.

Christian practice today offers us little help with crossing these thresholds, even when our journey passes through physical trauma such as miscarriage or a change in relationships like engagement to be married, events which fundamentally affect others as well. Our neglect of these landmark experiences in rites of passage and in Sunday worship shows how privatized our religion has become. Even children's literature is not afraid to explore this step. The overgrown door in Frances Hodgson Burnett's *The Secret Garden*, the hidden wardrobe door in C. S. Lewis' *The Lion, the Witch, and the Wardrobe* or Harry Potter's invisible platform all tell us what we ought to know from the Exodus or Christ's paschal journey: that daring to cross the threshold can open up a new promise of life beyond our imagination, a promise bringing dangers but also healing of neglect and grief.

The ending of the Sabbath is this kind of liminal experience. The story of God creating light out of darkness in creation is interwoven with our own journey back into the working week. As we hear the promise at the close of Shabbat, there is the hope that God's revelation will illuminate the coming days.

> Blessed shall you be in the city,
>   and blessed shall you be in the field.
> Blessed shall you be when you come in,
>   and blessed shall you be when you go out.
>   *Deuteronomy 28.3, 6*

Shabbat concludes with the ceremony of Havdalah, marking the separation of the holy day from the secular week. It centres on symbols of wine, sweet-smelling spices and a plaited candle, representing our desire to prolong the beauty of the day, a sense of loss at its passing and a wish for its fragrance to continue into the coming week. Rabbi Lee Wax suggests this ritual as a way of marking the beginning of menstruation with its separation of childhood and womanhood, loss and promise, continuity and discontinuity, and such a ritual could meet other pastoral needs as well.[22]

When we place such personal experiences before the presence of God they are drawn into what Rabbi Sylvia Rothschild calls 'a blend of Creation and Exodus, of particular and general, of what is and what could be' and we may use these states 'to create the dynamic and the journey both into the central moment and then back out into the world'. Her ritual for the loss of a baby is a poignant commemoration of this interweaving of the potential and actual, recognizing that God has taken away with their child the parents' hopes and happiness and, as they are unable to guide their child further, they ask for God to show mercy and compassion on them all. But the psalm texts which open and close the ritual not only make us aware of God at such an ending to life but of the God who accompanies us on a journey beyond grief when we thought there was no way ahead.

> Blessed is the one who comes in the name of God,
> we bless you from the house of God . . .
>
> You guard us when we go out and when we come in.
> In the shadow of your wings you shelter us.[23]

These words from the close of Jewish daily evening prayer take us back to Psalm 121 which in various traditions may mark the end of a day, the end of a pilgrimage or of life itself but always in the company of the God who makes all things new. So Anglican Fransiscans turn to the psalm when 'praying our farewells' to someone leaving a local community and express God's protecting presence as each person makes the sign of the cross on the forehead of the one leaving. When we face bereavement and the daunting threshold of a door into an empty house, we need the knowledge of God alongside us.

> Lord, be with us as we open the door.
> Come in with us, go out with us.
> Do not sleep when we sleep,
> but watch over us, protect us and keep us safe,
> our only helper and maker.
>
> cf. *Psalm 121* (*Prayers at home before the Funeral*,
> Common Worship)

The Psalmist's assurance has also been used in marriage services, especially for the bride and groom's walk to the altar, leaving behind family and friends in this recognition of the unique path on which they are embarking together before God.

This hymn of faith brings a blessing for the individual but it is a pilgrim psalm intended for those who know that their life is bound up with the journey of others. And its promise from God holds good not just for funerals and weddings but for any threshold we have to cross; a new relationship, a new enterprise at work or literally the move into a new home, even perhaps a visit to the dentist! We see the mountains around us, elements of life which are inspiring and challenging but potentially dangerous and recall that every extreme of heaven and earth, heat and cold, hope and fear, and all that lies between is in the hands of our Maker. God not only makes all things but promises to sustain and keep us, watching over us. On the new path where we find ourselves God does not allow our foot to stumble as we hit unexpected obstacles but protects us on our most vulnerable side – the right-hand side of the body being the part where the soldier is unprotected by the shield in his left hand.[24]

Such promised protection, especially in travel or combat, is found in the Celtic tradition of the spiritual breastplate (*lorica, llúirig*) with which believers gird themselves. These prayers may have originated in primitive prophylactic charms: Psalm 121, indeed, assures us that we will be guarded both from sunstroke and the astrological influence of the moon. The breastplate prayer influenced Anglo-Saxon meditations on the passion and developed a whole spirituality seeking protection for various parts of the body by appealing to the redeeming limbs of the crucified Christ.[25] Our psalm also finds God encompassing our eyes, feet and hands. Above all, amidst comings and goings with all the stress of change and uncertainty, the hopes and doubts about opportunities being fulfilled, the loves and fears for those sharing our journey, we may depend on the God who is our guide and guard for ever.

> I lift up my eyes to the hills:
>> from where shall come my help?
> My help comes from the Lord,
>> Maker of heaven and earth.

17

The Lord will not let your foot slip,
   your guardian will not slumber.
See, no slumber nor sleeping
   delays the guardian of Israel.
The Lord will be your guardian
   and be shielding your right hand.
By day the sun shall not strike you,
   nor yet the moon by night.
The Lord shall guard you from all harm,
   and be ever guarding your life.
The Lord shall guard your going and coming,
   from this time forth and evermore.

Second Sight

Sacred space

Places often have a vivid meaning for us, helping us to locate experiences in our memory and giving them perspective. There is the place where we first met our lover, the walk we take on holiday with the family, a garden to which we return for healing when hurt, or a favourite corner of the room where a much loved relative sat. And, just as in ikon painting bodily proportions do not correspond to actual measurements but to a spiritual dimension, so our recollection of these places is coloured by their meaning for us rather than any geographical accuracy.

In this light we can understand the importance of Jerusalem, where God revealed to a particular people a purpose for the whole world. That meeting-place of heaven and earth was the Temple of the Lord. This image of greatness is found in Temple psalmody as it was in its architecture. Drawing on the mythology of other cultic sites, the psalmist sings:

> Great is the Lord and greatly to be praised:
>   in the city of our God, the mountain of God's holy
>   place.
> High and beautiful, joy of all the earth,
>   Mount Zion, heart of the north,
>   it is the city of the great King.
>
> *Psalm 48.1–2*

The praises of Baal's northern sanctuary have been relocated to Zion, a move perhaps represented by the bronze pillars placed near the Temple entrance, symbolizing the mountains which flanked the approach to the Temple of Baal (1 Kings 7.15, 21). The Ugaritic mountain of paradise becomes the garden of Eden (Ezek. 28.13–14). Gihon, the primeval river of paradise, reappears as the Temple's sacred spring, 'a river whose streams make glad the city of God' (Gen. 2.13; Ps. 46.4).

As these primitive places were moved theologically to Jerusalem, so Jews later transferred the idea of sacred space to the synagogue or the home once they no longer had access to the Temple, a process which had already begun in exile with their worship by the waters of Babylon (Ps. 137 cf. Ezek. 1.1). Likewise, Christians moved the sacred route of Jesus' passion and made their own Stations of the Cross in the local church or named a porch to receive penitents after the Galilee, evoking through font and water-stoup the waters where the disciples heard his call and struggled for faith. The Ethiopians even called the Blue Nile their own Gihon. Hospitals like Bethlehem or Bedlam sought to recall the place of God's incarnation. In Wales and North America the whole landscape is claimed as a promised land by naming communities after the holy places of God's people: Tabor, Shiloh, Siloam and Bethel.

Jerusalem itself has become a symbol among African independent churches which have renamed the villages of their founding prophets, such as Simon Kimbangu's Nkamba-Jerusalem in Zaire or Alice Lenshina's Mount Zion in Zambia. These focal points are often the scene of massive baptismal and purification rites in sacred waters, replicating the biblical Zion.[1] The Celtic legend of Joseph of Arimathea bringing Christ to Glastonbury still expresses the longing of many people, including New Age worshippers, to rediscover God on home ground.

The attraction of holy places reveals our anxiety that we are losing our roots and our identity in a bland world of global media and market forces. People in villages may still have a link with places of worship because of the churchyard but the urban church is often only open on Sundays and the departed are cremated miles away from the locality. 'The religion of the unchurched has not disappeared so much as been relocated to a private sphere which is not accessible or visible to interested outsiders, including pastors.'[2]

The struggle to see

The Church bears some blame for this. When people have wanted to share the mystery of birth, love or death, they have sometimes been offered the cold stones of rationalism. The militant catholic tendency has wanted to hedge around the purity of the sacraments by excluding the morally dubious, and muscular evangelicals have erected hurdles for others to jump over and prove their faith. Minimalist liberals have denuded our spiritual landscape and smoothed over the raw challenges of Scripture. We offer wordy service-sheets and overhead projectors but do people see a vision of God in the liturgy? Do we no longer believe that we can meet God through the Gospel story told in book or stone, through the sacred space of the church, or the visible movement and matter of the sacraments?

Larry Hoffmann, a Jewish liturgist, reminds us that, just as in drama the cauldron in *Macbeth* or the balcony in *Romeo and Juliet* are hardly disposable props, so liturgical symbols need to be clearly seen without being overloaded by extraneous decor or text:

> Mere words will probably be perceived as sign. But more often than not, the colours, sounds, and objects that surround the words are what actually symbolize for people; it is things like the shofar, the candles, the white vestments, or some other object specific to the day's liturgy that people will remember from their childhood. The children present today will remember these items in the future, far after the specific words of prayer have been uttered, heard, and forgotten.[3]

Our need for this visible encounter survived various attempts to suppress it long before iconoclasm or the Reformation. The warnings in the Torah that no one shall see the Lord and live were circumvented by scribes using an intermediary angel of the Lord to appear and speak for God. They altered the text where

people had seen God so that they appeared before God rather
than God appear to them (Exod. 23.17, 25; 1 Sam. 1.22;
Pss. 42.3, 84.7; Job 33.26).[4] But a more primitive religious
experience won through. After the binding of Isaac, the Greek
text insists that 'on the mountain of the Lord, God is seen' and
when Jacob wrestles by the waters of Jabbok with a man who
will give him no name but offers a blessing, he declares, 'I have
seen God face to face and yet my life is preserved' (Gen. 22.14;
32.30). In the wilderness the people offer their sacrifice to the
Lord while Moses and the elders ascend Mount Sinai to
commune with God.

> And they saw the God of Israel, under whose feet there was
> something like a pavement of sapphire stone, like the very
> heaven for clearness. God did not lay a hand on the chiefs
> of the people of Israel, and they gazed upon God and ate
> and drank.
>
> *Exodus 24.10–11*

The word 'gaze' (*haza*) here suggests not a spectacle but an
experience of contemplation. It often describes leaders or prophets apprehending God in a dream or vision or the particular
role of a seer in the worshipping community (Gen. 15.1, 22;
Num. 24.4; Isa. 1.1; Ezek. 12.27; Amos 1.1). Music was a
medium of this prophetic and contemplative ministry: the chron-
icler describes Heman, Asaph and Jeduthun (all connected with
the Psalter) as seers, whose sons accompanied themselves
with lyre, harp and cymbals, prophesying in praise of God (1
Chron. 25.1–8; 2 Chron. 29.30; 35.15). Such revelations in
worship go back to the Torah: Abram receives his night vision
after he had offered sacrifice, torched by God's terrifying fire in
the darkness. At the binding of Isaac and with the elders at
Sinai the Lord is seen at the time of sacrifice. For prophets like
Micaiah, Isaiah or the priest Ezekiel the worship of the Lord of
hosts was the time of encounter when they saw the Lord in
heavenly glory and received their call. A more contemplative
Church is likely to allow seekers to find and vocations to be heard
in our own day.

Contemplation also gives an insight into the justice of God,

even when we are surrounded by violence and evil. The presence
of God is an assurance that God does scrutinize human motives
and offers the strength of communion and the faith that good will
prevail.

> The Lord is in his holy temple,
>   the Lord, whose throne is in heaven,
> whose eyes gaze, whose piercing look
>   tests the children of earth.
> For the Lord is righteous and loves righteous deeds:
>   the upright shall gaze upon God's face.
>
> *Psalm 11.4, 7*

The righteous will see God's justice vindicated even if it be in
the re-awakening after death (Pss. 58.10; 17.15).

Such prayer sustains us through the most difficult times and
brings hope when our view is clouded by despair. In his flight
from Saul, in a wilderness of earth and heart, what encourages
David is the remembrance of communion with God in worship.

> O God, you are my God, at first light I look for you;
>   my soul thirsts for you, my flesh faints for you
>   in a dry and weary land where there is no water.
> At such times I have gazed upon you in the sanctuary
>   to see your power and your glory.
>
> *Psalm 63.1–2*

As with Jacob at the Jabbok river, this is not a sudden revelation but strength drawn from a struggle for faith. The word 'look
for' (in Hebrew *'ashaherecha* cf. *shahar* – dawn or dark) suggests
that we are searching for what we know is near but struggle to
find in the half-dark, half-light of dawn. The Greek and Latin
translations (*orthrizo, de luce vigilo*) similarly disposed this psalm
for Matins. Commenting on these verses, Dag Hammarskjöld
understood the paradox of a mature relationship with God who
is near yet far, whose look is 'a shy caress', for the Lover desires
for the beloved a perfection, which requires the independence of
the beloved.[5] It may seem that God is hard to reach, but this is a
love which liberates, not dominates, and allows us to form
a relationship in freedom.

The counterpart to our search is God's readiness to be found. The psalms declare that it is in Judah where God has a dwelling-place. God is revealed on the holy mountain, shining forth from the beauty of the sanctuary so that salvation may be displayed before the nations (Pss. 76, 48, 50, 98). Worshippers understood this experience as a visual encounter.

> One thing I have asked of the Lord, which I long for:
> may I dwell in the house of the Lord all the days of
> my life
> to gaze on your beauty, O Lord, and seek you in
> your temple.
>
> *Psalm 27.4*

Walking the wilderness

A holy place, therefore, is not primarily a picturesque piece of landscape or an ancient building but a place where people have prayed and struggled and where our search can be fruitfully and safely explored in a community of faith. Others travel with us through pain and joy and pray with us when we cannot. The psalms help us to cross emotional and spiritual territory together, whether we make our journey to the font, the altar or the grave. We need ritual movement to survive and transform these experiences. Portable fonts and altars may be convenient but they sometimes miss the point that it is we who have to make the move if we are to mature. Contemplation and communion are not static: they lead us 'from glory to glory advancing'.

> To follow wherever God may lead is to see God, whose passing by is a sign of God's presence for the one who follows.[6]

Psalm 23 is used in all rites of passage but it offers an especially illuminating insight into baptism. Its influence on the iconography of baptisteries can be traced from the painting of the Good Shepherd beside the font of the third-century Syrian house-church at Dura Europos to Victorian stained-glass.

At the outset of the psalm we meet 'my shepherding Lord'

(the participial form is not reflected in translations), moving the flock on to waters which are safe, clear and accessible. The intensive form of the verb 'revive' suggests that the shepherd is always looking out for our welfare, repeatedly turning us in the right direction; a reminder that baptism is only the beginning of a journey on which we shall be challenged again and again to follow Christ's lead. In a nomadic economy where pastures are over-grazed and water-courses change with the seasons, sheep cannot always remain in the same place or they die – a truth lost on some stalwart Christians! The paths of righteousness are not just correct moral rules to keep but ways that will engender justice for the whole community. The derivation of the word 'paths' (*ma'ggle*) from 'round' (*'agol*) implies a liturgical procession which would have been led by the anointed sovereign with crook and staff (orb and sceptre) showing God's authority. By our baptism we share in that royal priesthood and join the same walk with Christ.

> Lord, you are my shepherd;
> there is nothing I shall want.
> Fresh and green are the pastures
> where you give me repose.
> Near restful waters you lead me,
> to revive my drooping spirit.
>
> You guide me along the right path:
> you are true to your name.
> If I should walk in the valley of darkness
> no evil would I fear.
> You are there with your crook and your staff;
> with these you give me comfort.
>
> You have prepared a banquet for me
> in the sight of my foes.
> My head you have anointed with oil;
> my cup is overflowing.
>
> Surely goodness and kindness shall follow me

all the days of my life.
In the Lord's own house shall I dwell
for ever and ever.

Roman Baptismal Lectionary

As we arrive at the waters of baptism (the door of the faithful to communion illustrated on many fonts by doves feeding from the vine) we look to the final banquet of God, prepared for our homecoming, but there is no attempt to avoid harsh realities; for all God's guidance, the enemy is still there. According to Jewish tradition, David prayed this psalm while taking refuge from his enemies in the dry wastes of the wilderness which God mercifully watered for him (1 Sam. 22.5). The table of plenty is prepared here in the very sight of our adversaries, even in spite of us, for the Latin version (*contra me*) suggests that the banquet not only refreshes us but confronts our own doubts, sins and fears. At the point of our own weakness we see the overwhelming grace of God set before us in this covenant meal to which we bring nothing but ourselves. Now we have a closer view of our enemies around us and within, but we see them with God's table of mercy interposed between them and us. We see them at last in the light of God.

The same realism pervades Psalms 42–43 which has long been associated with baptism. Its undercurrent of uncertainty makes it an appropriate hymn for both paschal mysteries of birth and death. The struggle is compared to that of the deer who hears the springs of water flowing and desperately tries to trace them beneath the rocks. Hearing is not enough: we must come face to face with the source for our thirst to be quenched.

As the deer longs for the water brooks,
so longs my soul for you, O God.
My soul is athirst for God, even for the living God;
when shall I come before the presence of God?
My tears have been my bread day and night,
while all day long they say to me, 'Where is now your
    God?'

Procession to the Font (Common Worship)

The symbol of water here is full of ambivalence. The desire for refreshing streams is taunted by tears welling up inside us and despair threatening to overwhelm us.

> Deep is calling on deep in the roar of waters.
> Your torrents and all your waves swept over me.
>
> *Roman Office of Readings for the Dead*

And the God, who is implicated in the waves, is seen not only to bear the ultimate responsibility but to share in the struggle with us. Lancelot Andrewes understood the turmoil of the waters as a profound dialogue with God: 'deep calls to deep, the deep of our pitifulness, the deep of your pitying heart'.[7] For the Dutch writer Etty Hillesum, who died at Auschwitz, the sense that God is present within us in our questionings helps us respond: 'And if I say that I hearken, it is really God who hearkens inside me, the most essential and the deepest in me hearkening to the most essential and the deepest in the other, God to God.' This awareness enabled her to change her vision of the world around her: she felt that she could not wait for the world to change to suit her; she must change the way she saw it. Her theology is a powerful testimony to liberation through discernment in a situation of utter powerlessness.[8]

In the psalm the despairing are encouraged to see their plight in the light of past experience, recalling the strength they found in worshipping together:

> These things will I remember
> as I pour out my soul:
> how I would lead a rejoicing crowd
> into the house of God.
>
> *Roman Easter Vigil*

Yet there is a suggestion amidst this nostalgia that they came to that celebration in weariness and perhaps with faltering faith. The Hebrew word 'lead' (*'edadem*) depicts a parent patiently guiding the halting steps of a toddler, and its reflexive form implies the leader had to gather the straggling worshippers around him, just as we have to collect our wandering thoughts for worship.

Western Christendom has tended to sidestep the emotional conflicts surrounding baptism, but Robin Green asks us to stay with that ambiguity of joy and pain. 'Because water is both a creative and destructive force, it puts human beings in touch with both sides of themselves. Requests for baptism may reflect this level of pastoral need . . . it may be these deep, irrational and unconscious forces that lead many people to ask for Christian baptism . . . There is something in the symbol of water that both threatens and promises. Pastors have to take hold of that ambiguity and use it creatively.'[9]

Seeing the unseen

What is it, then, that we see in the liturgy? A mirage or an oasis? Is the meaning really in the journey so that we can forget about the destination? Such a long distance between reality and fulfilment may suit many of us very well, excusing the gap between the two in our own Christian living. Yet here before us are real water, oil, light and a table prepared with bread and wine.

Those who first sang the psalms expected that God would be revealed in worship. The kind of symbolic actions in the liturgy were valid not just for the congregation but for the whole universe. Even deprived of Temple ritual, Ezekiel continued in exile to communicate God's power over world events through prophetic signs.

> All these acts suggest the 'make-believe' of a child . . . but the prophets were able to enter their kingdom just because in some respects they were children, and could take the 'make-believe' so seriously. Through these trivialities (as we call them) they were conscious of exerting a power over outer events . . .[10]

They know no distinction between time and eternity: the Lord is in the holy temple, the Lord is enthroned in heaven (Ezek. 11.4). In Rabbinic literature, the Ark is as dear to God as the Seat of Glory above and the worship offered on earth corresponds to that in heaven. 'In the days when the Temple existed, the High

Priest sacrificed and burned incense in the lower Temple, and the
Archangel, Michael the High Priest, stood opposite him and
sacrificed and burned incense in the upper Temple.' The two
worlds are so united in worship that 'when that of below is built
anew, this of above will be built anew.'[11] Jesus himself recognizes
that our worship influences heaven when he speaks of a sinner's
repentance bringing joy to the angels (Luke 15.10).

We also believe that in worship we enter a realm where God
is known in power. Without that revelation it is impertinent to
think that we have anything to offer the world. The Byzantine
Liturgy begins by proclaiming 'Blessed is the kingdom of the
Father, and of the Son, and of the Holy Spirit, now and for ever
and to the ages of ages.' Alexander Schmemann taught that the
very joy of our Easter faith is that in the liturgy we experience
the age to come in our midst: our faith is already 'the substance
of things hoped for, the evidence of things not seen' (Heb. 11.1).
This determines our understanding of symbolism. People may
regard a symbol as the sign of an absent reality, whereas

> the purpose and function of the symbol is *not* to illustrate
> (this would presume the *absence* of what is illustrated) but
> rather to *manifest* and to *communicate* what is manifested. We
> might say that the symbol does not so much 'resemble' the
> reality that it symbolizes as it participates in it, and there-
> fore it is capable of communicating it in reality.[12]

One important moment of communication is the reading of
Scripture. Whether in the Ark of a synagogue, the open Bible
of a Reformed church or a Gospel procession, the Word is both
seen and heard. In the Temple, as in the synagogue today, the
Word of God was read from the scroll of the Law taken from
the Ark. The climax to the reading was the return of the Law to
its throne. Just as Christians respond to the Gospel with 'Glory
to you, Lord', implying that Christ and the Gospel are one, so
the Ark and the Lord are identified, the symbol sharing in the
reality:

> Rise up, Lord, to Your place of rest,
> You and the Ark of Your strength!
> *Psalm 132.8 (Sabbath Morning Service,* FPJW)

In a tradition dating from David, Psalm 29 is still sung as the Law is returned in praise of God's universal Word. The wings of the cherubim represented the clouds illuminated with lightning that heralded the Lord's voice at Sinai. The Lord appeared in the beauty of the holy apparel on the Ark whose blue cloth represented heaven while the cry of 'Glory' responded to the song of the angels. The echoing of the Lord's voice over the waters may refer to a procession, for the Temple courtyard had white and blue marble walls to suggest the waves of the sea.[13] The Word proclaimed and processed displayed God's sovereignty over every element of the cosmos.

> Worship the Lord in the beauty of holiness!
> The voice of the Lord echoes over the waters,
> the God of glory thunders,
> the Lord is echoing over the mighty waters.
> The voice of the Lord in power,
> the voice of the Lord in majesty!
> (*Sabbath Morning Service*, FPJW)

The Ark was also often associated with the perpetual light of the sevenfold golden Menorah, a symbol of God's presence (1 Sam. 3.3; Pss. 36.9; 80.1–3; 132.8, 17) and the sense of awe pertaining to this lampstand can be gathered from the prohibition against making any copy of the sacred one in the Temple and the interpretation of its flaming lights as the eyes of the Lord.[14] The Lord is indeed light (Zech. 4.10; Ps. 27.1). Psalm 27 shows that this revelation came not just from the symbol of light but from the sacrifice when God's will was sought (*biker*), a ritual term for scrutinizing omens. The power of God was manifested through the Word of the Ark, the light of the lampstand and the altar of sacrifice but also through dramatic rituals using a molten sea for cosmic battles (1 Kings 7.23–6). Psalm 46 sets before us such a liturgy where we may witness God's saving power.

> Come now and look upon the works of the Lord,
> who has done such awesome things on earth.
> It is God who makes war to cease in all the world,

breaking the bow and shattering the spear
and burning the shields with fire.

Symbolic spears are shattered and shields burnt before the prophetic voice finally silences the battle, declaring:

Be still, then, and know that I am God:
I will be exalted among the nations;
I will be exalted in the earth.

More explicit is the invasion of pagan kings overwhelming Jerusalem like a flood, perhaps symbolized with some water ritual. Certainly the verb *dimminu* ('displayed') suggests making a likeness:

As we have heard, so we have seen
in the city of the Lord of hosts, in the city of our God.
May God establish it for ever. Selah!
We have displayed your faithful love, O God
in the womb of your Temple.

Psalm 48.8–9

If we are tempted to think that such cosmic themes could hardly be interpreted in drama, we have only to reflect on how Christians symbolize the sacrifice of Christ on the cross with bread and wine.

The waters of rebirth

As the liturgy celebrates this divine purpose for the world, we realize that God's perception of us is more generous than our own anxious self-image. Our communion with the Maker and Lover of all can only make us grow in awareness of the hope and joy God longs for us to discover.

O send forth your light and your truth;
let these be my guide.
Let them bring me to your holy mountain,
to the place where you dwell.
And I will come to your altar, O God,
the God of my joy.

Psalm 43 (Roman Easter Vigil)

The Iona Community imaginatively uses these verses in four 'exodus liturgies', sung as people move from one area of the church to another, representing our journey through aspects of human experience such as adolescence or bereavement and reminding us that we are led across this terrain to find ourselves in the light of God. Such enlightenment was at the heart of Jesus' baptism. The Jordan waters were not waters of recognition for John alone, but for Jesus 'they were "waters of awakening", the moment when he awoke, as it were, to his true "Self".'[15]

In the psalms the pilgrimage of worship is the path to the source of life itself. Among other religious traditions, the natives of Easter Island named their home 'the navel of the world' after the stone which their prolific founder had brought there. The Greeks described the round stone at Delphi as 'the midmost navel of fair-forested mother-earth'. Aborigines regard the sacred rock of Uluru as the *wangigit* (navel) of the earth and the Maori meeting house is sometimes called the *poho* (bosom) of the ancestor. So the priests of Jerusalem could speak of their people living on the navel of the earth (Ezek. 38.12), a rock forming the floor of the Holy of Holies, said to be the first solid thing that God created amidst the primeval waters.[16]

Maternal imagery is also used for the stone at the base of the altar, where communion feasts were celebrated above the 'breast' (*ḥiku*) of the earth (Ezek. 43.13–14). In the liturgy God is present in the midst, or we may translate the belly or womb of the Temple (Pss. 48.9; 74.4).

It is the Lord who comes to dwell in the womb of daughter Israel renewing her in love and finding joy in her (Zeph. 3.14–17). We see the sanctuary as a birthplace, imitating the swallow who nests at the altar to lay her young (Ps. 84.3). Those who catechized candidates for baptism in the Early Church saw in the waters of the font a model of God's mothering, bringing us to new birth. 'For just as whoever is in the dark cannot see but whoever is in daylight remains in the light, so in descending as in the dark, you saw nothing, but in ascending again, you found yourselves to be as in daylight. And in that moment, you died and were born, and that water of salvation became for you both tomb and mother.'[17]

When the images of rebirth and feeding are brought together, we begin to understand the Church not as a mechanical organization but a growing organism. In a Persian church manual of the late fourth century, both the liturgy and the worshippers help the church to be the mother of all who are baptized.

> This church, with its altar and baptism, gives birth to men and women as children, and they suck her milk until they are weaned. Then they come to growth and to knowledge that belongs both to the body and to the heart, whereupon they make their bodies temples and their hearts altars . . .[18]

In the psalms the worshipping community encounters the parental dependability of God whose love, even in an age of violence and corruption, enlightens us as we are nurtured. The early medieval Fang-shan cross from northern China focuses spiritual illumination and growth on the grace of God with a lotus blossoming from the root of the cross and the Syriac text of Psalm 34: 'Look to him and hope in him'. Another text, rich in imagery for a baptismal liturgy, celebrates God as source of life, light and nourishment with a homonym in the Hebrew recalling the promise of the garden of Eden:

> How precious, Lord, your faithful love,
>   Earth's children seek safe-keeping,
> Your house shall feed them to the full,
>   From Eden's river drinking.
> Life, life, is flowing free,
>   With you we find the well of life.
> Light, light, in you we see,
>   Your love at length fulfilling.
>   *Baptism Processional* cf. *Psalm 36 (T. Greensleeves)*

The linking of water and light suggests reflection but also revelation and rebirth. The word 'well' (*makor*) is used both of the eye as the source of light and the source of menstruation (Jer. 9.1; Lev. 12.7; 20.18) while the eye (*'ayin*) can be a fountain as well as a wife, the spring from which the husband drinks (Ps. 68.26: Prov. 5.18). The symbolism is developed by Ephrem in his picture of the merchant who is drunk with love and dives into the waters to uncover the pearl of the Eucharist, not to make her naked, for her nakedness is clothed in light.[19] In the writings of medieval mystics Mary is often celebrated as the crystal immersed in water through which shone the blazing sun of God, and the dedication of wells and riverside churches to Our Lady may be traced on the landscape. In the womb of the Temple our longing is fulfilled, our union with God restored, new vocations are revealed, relationships reborn, and we see creation around us in the light of God.

A world view

Liturgy should change the way we look at the world and the value we place on its resources, for God has chosen the material world to communicate grace and goodness. 'The regenerate person . . . will move with reverence in the created world, seeing it illumined with the divine light that fills the sky, the earth and all that exists. He will venerate everything not on account of itself but because it is a receptacle of divine energy.'[20] In a climate of international fear and threat, 'there is a river whose streams make glad the city of God'; and people find faith in worship to believe that God can bring peace (Ps. 46). From the feast of Sukkot (Tabernacles) with its libations of water, Ezekiel develops his final apocalyptic vision where water flows from the altar through the Temple towards the Messianic east, bringing fresh water instead of stagnant with abundance of fish and trees bearing fruit for food and leaves for healing. The same feast inspires Jesus to see himself as the source of the Spirit's living water, declaring, 'Out of this womb shall streams of living water flow' (Ezek. 47; John 7.38).

The common practice of isolating baptism from the Eucharist has blocked our vision from font to altar, obscuring a proper theology of God as Creator, Sustainer and End of all and terminating rather than nurturing people's progress in the spiritual life. The absence of baptism from the congregation has blinded us to fundamental decisions in discipleship and made the Eucharist a personal refreshment stop, not a journey to the paradise of God. Michaelangelo painted a truer theology of the Eucharist on the

Sistine Chapel ceiling with the scenes from Genesis apparently in reverse order, beginning with the drunkenness of Noah at the entrance and progressing to the creation over the altar.

If our sacramental life is to be a universal blessing, we will need to see our worship in a broader context. For the Psalmist, the Temple was the source of life for all peoples:

> Of the holy city it shall be said, 'Everyone was born in her',
>   and it is the Most High who shall sustain her.
> Registering the nations, the Lord shall record,
>   'This one was born there.'
> Singers and dancers shall say,
>   'All my fresh springs are in you.'
>
> *Psalm 87*

Transformed by our baptism to be 'the sap of the world,'[21] we may become like the Indian painter Jyoti Sahi's woman at the well. As she draws the living waters from the very heart of Christ, gazing into his eyes, her body seems to become like a flowing river, running into the parched earth beneath her feet.[22] An early Greek preacher once challenged his congregation at Epiphany:

> Come, all tribes of nations . . . This is the water which partakes of the Spirit, it waters paradise, it causes the earth to drink, it makes the plants to grow. In a word, it regenerates human beings by causing them to be reborn . . . I want to go back to the fountain of life and cause the stream of all remedies to break forth.[23]

This transfiguring vision appears in the baptistery of a church on Mount Nebo in Jordan. Beside the font a mosaic depicts shepherds and hunters fighting lions and bears but the scene changes to a world where animals and farmers cooperate with each other and forage among the fruit-laden trees. Wherever the waters of baptism flow, in a hospital ward, on a deprived housing estate or the most affluent commuter village, God is seen and touched, outsiders are welcomed, the vulnerable and powerful share each other's strengths and weaknesses and people are changed. Whatever its infamy or anonymity, that place is now seen to be the kingdom of God.

THREE

The Call of Love

Partner in love

A journey can be just the chance for someone to bore their
captive audience with some tedious tale. Even an outing with
children whom we dearly love arouses our worst reactions when
they pass the time winding each other up. But travelling with a
supportive friend, an engaging stranger or a partner with whom
we never have enough time, is a pleasure.

Such a companion is how our forebears found the Word of
God. Throughout that great hymn of praise on the Word, Psalm
119, the Law is celebrated as 'my delight' (*sha'ashu'ay*), someone
close to us who plays with us and gives us pleasure, a companion
and counsellor.

> Your statutes have become songs for me,
>   wherever I make my home on my travels.
> How I have come to love your law!
>   All the day long she has been the one I have thought of.
> *Psalm 119.54, 97*

The Psalmist understands that this love is a mutual delight, for
God finds as much joy in being in our company.

> The Lord has brought me out into an open place,
>   setting me free, because God found pleasure in me.
> *Psalm 18.19*

One spiritual director has used this liberating verse to

encourage those who come to her, because, when we begin
to explore how God may be finding delight in our play and
pleasure, we experience God as a different kind of person from
the harsh stereotype we project and we are freed to be
ourselves.[1]

Even the Book of Psalms itself can become a physical companion. One medieval Irish monk, who loses his Psalter to four
others borrowing it in turn, greets its return as a lover coming
home to a neglectful partner:

> Crinoc, lady of measured melody,
>> not young, but with modest maiden mind,
> together once in Niall's northern land
>> we slept, we two, as man and womankind . . .
>
> Seeking the presence of elusive God,
>> wandering we stray, but the way is found,
> following the mighty melodies that with you
>> throughout the pathways of the world resound.[2]

In Jewish literature the Word or Wisdom of God appears as
the feminine persona of God, continually participating in the
work of divine grace, 'God's daily delight, rejoicing in the
inhabited world and delighting in the human race' (Prov.
8.30–31). This creative relationship is depicted with sexual
imagery, whether it be the bridegroom bounding out of the
marriage-bed with joy or the taste of honey, milk or wine under
the lover's tongue. The female gender of the word Torah (Law) is
given fullest expression in one tradition of Judaism on the Feast
of Tabernacles when the bonding of Word and worshipper is
demonstrated as each dances with a Torah scroll as their partner.[3]
The feminine aspect of wisdom words in Hebrew also brings to
the psalms insight into our intimate relationship with God.

> The heavens are telling God's glorious story,
>> God's handiwork has its heralds above;
> There shines the sun like a bridegroom in glory,
>> Coming with joy from the fervour of love.

The Law of the Lord is embracing creation,
    True is God's pledge, turning simple to wise;
She will be bringing our soul restoration,
    Bright her command, giving light to the eyes.

Her reverence of God is for ever our cleansing,
    Justice and truth all together unite.
Greater than gold, she deserves our desiring,
    Sweeter than honey, she is our delight.

You counsel me, Lord, with your guidance and gladness,
    See, I am yours: your salvation impart.
O let your womb be o'erflowing with tenderness,
    May I find life with your Word in my heart.
              Psalms 19.1–10; 119.24, 94, 77 (Tune: Was lebet)

The call of the beloved

The voice of God is the other, the lover who finds in us what we
cannot discover for ourselves. In the world of the Psalmist this
awareness of the numinous was often born out of hours of
continuous prayer. The words used for meditation (*hagah, siaḥ*)
evoke the low, murmuring sound of chanting.

> In the Law of the Lord they find their delight,
>   and upon the Law they chant their meditation day and
>   night.
>   *Psalm 1.2; cf. 35.28; 119.97*

The music itself is not to be a distraction: it is God's word,
learned and contemplated, that gives the Psalmist a melody of
meaning for life (Ps. 119.54). The oracles of the prophets are
often introduced with the telling phrase *n'um'Adonai*, suggesting
a sighing or whispering from the Lord during a period of contemplation.[4] Verses from the psalms paint a picture of the
prophet or priest praying through the night, sustained by
the interweaving of silence and music during which the same
thought from God reoccurs.

I remember the music I played in the night,
    with my heart I meditate and search my spirit.

Psalm 77.6

The role of music is to call us to worship God, this partner in creation who seeks our presence. Psalm 95 has always had a place in liturgy, inviting people to meet with God. Already in the mid-fourth century among the monastic houses founded by Pacho-mios at Tabennesi in the Nile valley, the psalm was being used to inspire awe and penitence: 'When once we are prostrate on our face, let us weep in our heart for our sins, as it is written, "Come, let us adore and weep before the Lord our Maker".'[5] A century later the psalm appears as an invitatory to prayer in the monasteries of Italy. In the Byzantine rite the call at Vespers 'Come, let us worship and bow down before our Sovereign God' prepares the congregation for the procession of light and the offering of incense acclaiming God's presence among them. Later, these verses became part of the opening procession at the Eucharist and now accompany the Little Entrance as the Gospel is brought forth.

Come, let us sing for joy to the Lord,
    let us shout for joy to God our Saviour.
Let us come before God's face with thanksgiving,
    let us shout to God in psalms of praise!
For God is a great Lord,
    and a great Sovereign over all the earth!

Liturgy of St John Chrysostom

For Orthodox, the face of God in the psalm is that of the Saviour born in the form of a servant, but his vulnerable humility only enhances our awe of Christ as Lord of all.[6]

Celebrating the incarnate Christ, the Western Church turned to the same words. They seemed to capture the adoration of the first visitors to the manger, especially as people were used to seeing Benedictine monks genuflecting during the responses of Psalm 95 at Matins. So the daily liturgical practice of the Divine Office was carried straight into the world of drama. The stage directions of the Fleury Play of Herod (*c.* 1 200) set the scene, including audience participation:

> Then the shepherds, throwing themselves to the ground, shall worship the child, singing, 'Blessed be the King of ages'. Afterwards, rising up, they shall invite those present to worship the child, singing three times:
> *Venite, venite, adoremus Deum, qui ipse est Salvator noster.*
> Come, come, let us worship God, who indeed is our Saviour.[7]

Perhaps our own nativity plays should invite parents to adore the Saviour rather than their children! We even have a suitable carol, for it seems that this Matins antiphon influenced the chorus of 'O come, all ye faithful' whose earliest manuscript (*c.* 1 740) *Venite, adorate* was later changed to correspond with the words of Psalm 95.

Worship that is just entertainment or only framed to meet the immediate needs of the consumer will fail. Only where we make space for another, silence to sense their presence and hear their voice, can we lose ourselves in the encounter of love and discover the wonder of the person being revealed to us.

Change of direction

There is a long tradition of prophets, who were mainly drawn from priestly orders, receiving their calling during worship. Jahaziel the Levite is filled with the Spirit of the Lord in a service of penitence. Micaiah hears God calling him in a vision of the heavenly host and likewise Isaiah hears the Lord's voice amidst the offering of incense at the procession of the Ark. Even after the destruction of the Temple in the trauma of exile, Ezekiel sees a vision of God borne on the wings of living creatures like the Ark on the cherubim and is overwhelmed by God's mission for him (2 Chron. 20.3–19; 1 Kings 22.19–23; Isa. 6; Ezek. 1–2). Such encounters are worlds away from the Western Church with its often anodyne worship and pastoral sermons which avoid the faintest whiff of controversy. Ours is worship for a private world of personal stereos, selected videos and mobile phones where we each fill our own space with things we choose to hear, deaf to the cry of others or the call of God.

The prophetic singers of the psalms had a vocation to help the whole community hear God's message. Strategically placed on fifteen semi-circular steps in the Temple between the courts reserved for men and women,[8] they took their place on the threshold of the world and the sanctuary, mediating in song the needs of the people to God and the saving help of God to the world. The title of the guild of Asaph in particular suggests a connection with exorcistic healing and divination by dreams and other signs in the tradition of Joseph.[9] Music is a powerful medium for gathering together a congregation's intercessions as well as communicating the prophetic. Those who lead worship in song should realize not only the role of music in the liturgy but their own liminal position between congregation and sanctuary. The word of the prophetic preacher also belongs to the worshipping community. Even such a defender and martyr for the poor as Oscar Romero of El Salvador could say, 'I've never felt I was a prophet as an individual. No, it's you and I, the people of God, who are a prophetic people.'[10]

Often we have to be shaken out of habit or apathy to heed God's call. 'I hear a voice I had not known' (Ps. 81.5), the Psalmist ironically declares to a congregation that has forgotten God amongst its new idols. The Church has begun to rescue Advent from the kitsch of Christmas but still its message of changing direction lies latent. Psalm 50, which summons Jews to repentance on the Day of Atonement, makes a timely appearance in some Advent liturgies with God's demand for justice and truth. The challenge is directed at those who only come to worship at festivals!

> Our God is coming, and will not keep silence:
>   before you, O God, runs a consuming fire,
>   and a mighty tempest rages about you.
> You call on the heavens above, and on the earth below
>   to witness the judgment of your people.
> 'Gather my people before me,
>   the people who made covenant with me by sacrifice.'
>   *Advent Gradual* (A New Zealand Prayer Book)

Religion which is only practised at church festivals or on family occasions is an unusual, if welcome, interruption in the routine of life, where God apparently has nothing to say and is not required. God, however, seeks to speak to us day by day in unexpected and unsought situations, as the acclamation for the Lenten Gospel reminds us:

> The Lord is a great God.
> O that today you would listen to his voice.
> Harden not your hearts.
>
> *Psalm 95* (Common Worship)

A story in the Talmud tells how Rabbi Yoshua ben Levi came upon Elijah one day and asked him when the Messiah would come. Elijah told him to go and ask him himself. 'Where is he?', asked the Rabbi. 'Sitting at the gate of the city.' 'And how shall I know him?' asked the Rabbi. Elijah replied, 'He is sitting among the lepers covered with wounds. The others unbind all their wounds at the same time and then bind them up again, but he unbinds them one at a time and binds it up again, saying to himself, "Perhaps I shall be needed: if so, I must always be ready so as not to delay for a moment." ' Rabbi Yoshua asks the Messiah when the Master will come and he replies, 'Today'. Reporting this reply to Elijah, the Rabbi complains that the Messiah has deceived him, for he has not come today. Elijah reminds him, 'This is what he told you: "Today if you would listen to His voice." '[11]

Jews and Christians have found these words valuable for morning prayer, a call to come face to face with God, making a fresh start at the beginning of a new day, for every day may be the beginning of salvation for us or through us for others.

Promises for the beloved

Through the dialogue of worship, the community of the Psalmist received hope and encouragement from God, often expressed as a spiritual light. The promise of God's presence may have been mediated through rituals of the Ark in procession with its golden cherubim gleaming in sunlight and clouded in incense, or watching dramatic representations of enemies routed or seeing the high priest turn to face them and give them God's blessing (cf. Pss. 80, 99, 48, 67, 118; Num. 6.24–6). The gaze of adoring love betokens a reciprocal relationship where lover and beloved attend to each other.

> Look to God and be flooded with light,
>   and your faces shall never grow pale . . .
> The eyes of the Lord look to the righteous,
>   and God's ears are open to their cry.
>
> *Psalm 34.5, 15*

In every generation worshippers continue to find the living God meet them with the assurance of love and justice through the psalms. The promise itself seems to strengthen our resolve to see justice done, as Ernesto Cardenal affirms in this prayer from the midst of poverty and torture:

> Smash their secret police, O Lord . . .
> that their military might may vanish without trace.
> You are the one who reigns for centuries.
> You hear the prayer of the humble
> and the weeping of the orphaned.
>
> cf. *Psalm 10.15–18*[12]

For Janet Morley, the night vigil of the prophet echoes the struggle of women praying in a Church which denies them wholeness, justice and sometimes even a voice at all:

> For the darkness of choosing
> when you give us the moment
> to speak, and act, and change,
> and we cannot know what we have set in motion,
> but we still have to take the risk,
> we praise you O God:
>   *For the darkness and the light are both alike to you.*
>
> cf. *Psalm 139.12*[13]

Psalm 85 sets before us a liturgy of call and response where the prophet appeals to God to heed the plight of land and people and keep faith with past promises.

People: *Let us see, O Lord, your mercy*
          and give us your saving help.
Cantor: I will hear what the Lord has to say,
          a voice that speaks of peace,
          peace for his people.
          Salvation is near for the God-fearing,
          and his glory will dwell in our land.

Roman Gradual for Advent 2

The oracle is a vision of God's blessings embracing each other like angels, but the beauty of the text should not obscure the fact that the promise involves our cooperation and obedience, as this prayer for the firstfruits of harvest makes clear.

It is an excellent thing to recognize the needs of others:
the poor, the stranger, the birds of the air.
   Mercy and truth are met together.
   Righteousness and peace have kissed each other.[14]

The course of God's purpose may conflict with our selfish priorities. The Jewish commentator Samson Raphael Hirsch imagines mercy and truth taking different roads, for loving mercy is sought by everyone but truth is shunned because it hurts. Only when both meet in our human thinking and actions can there be wholeness and peace.[15] In our agricultural crises this has a poignant message for politicians, farmers and consumers alike. The practice of mass food production has not been reconciled with compassion and integrity, with results for all to see. The Psalmist knows that this fusion of purpose cannot become real by some sudden miracle but requires a journey of growth personally and socially.

Truth shall spring up from the earth,
and righteousness shall look down from heaven.
Righteousness shall go before you,
and peace shall be a pathway for your feet.
   Advent Evening Canticle (Celebrating Common Prayer)

It is at funerals that reassurance from Scripture is most sought and the Judeo–Christian tradition has often turned to Psalm 103 at such times. The Psalmist recognizes the stark reality of our transient life, yet sees it against the horizon of God's faithful love. We are not pawns in some game of chance poised between life and death but held in love by the one who is our parent for ever. God is called our Father but the divine compassion and loving-kindness (*raḥmīm*), literally 'feelings from the womb', are the instinct of a mother. Many funeral rites shy away from the psalm's opening verses with their promise of the God who alone can forgive beyond the grave, but the Syrian Orthodox burial service celebrates this truth with the Alleluias that characterize all Orthodox funerals.

> Bless the Lord, O my soul, Hallelujah,
>   and all that is within me, bless his holy name.
> Bless the Lord, O my soul, Hallelujah,
>   and forget not all his benefits,
> Who forgives all your iniquities, Hallelujah,
>   who heals all your diseases,
> Who redeems your life from destruction, Hallelujah,
>   and crowns you with loving-kindness and tender
>   mercies.

The promise is not just for funerals. Day by day our prayer and God's response become interwoven so that, even while we are asking for forgiveness, the answer already seems to be on our lips.

> Almighty God, whose steadfast love is as great
> as the heavens are high above the earth,
> remove our sins from us,
> as far as the east is from the west . . .
>   *Psalm 103.11–12, Absolution* (Kenyan Liturgy)

The prayer of the psalms helped to shape Jesus' own message of the kingdom of God. The promise of salvation for the poor, rejoicing for those who weep, inheritance of the earth for the meek, food for the righteous and blessing for the merciful, a vision of God for the pure in heart and the assurance of future generations for peacemakers – all the Beatitudes have their roots in the Psalter.[16]

Fruits of love

These are not vague aspirations; God longs to see the promise fulfilled. The fruitfulness of God's companionship with us is depicted as Wisdom flowing like a channel watering a garden, drenching the flower beds and swelling like a river moving into the sea (Sirach 24). In Isaiah, Israel, represented by Jerusalem, is God's delight, giving joy like a bride to her groom, her land is 'married', and her breasts nurse and console all who love her (Isa. 62, 66). The fruitfulness of creation and marriage become symbols of the way we mature as the lovers of God. Even in modern liturgical revision these rich images have been neglected, indicating the alienation of urban-centred liturgy from symbols of creation and agriculture. The increasing interest in Celtic spirituality points to the need to redress this lack.

The Psalter begins with a celebration of those who delight in the Law of the Lord, often symbolized by water.

> They become like a tree, transplanted by streams of
>   water,
>   yielding its fruit in due season.
>
> *Psalm 1.3*

Concluding the Communion of Ash Wednesday in Western rites, these words mark an appropriate beginning for our journey in Lent as we seek to grow in a deepening relationship with God through feeding on the Scriptures.

In Judaism the imagery survives in the actual furnishings of the Ark. The wooden rollers which secure the Torah scrolls are known as the *'Etz Chaim* ('Tree of Life') and their silver head-pieces are shaped like the juicy pomegranates from which they take their name (*rimmonim*). For the most part, Christian worship has only developed this theme for the cross, despite Jesus – following John the Baptist – using the fruit of the good tree as a lesson for our discipleship and identifying himself with the vine, whose fruitful branches we are called to be (Matt. 7; John 15). The symbol of fruit is taken up by the apostles to encourage us to grow in holiness and justice, goodness and truth, love, joy and peace (Rom. 6.22; Gal. 5.22; Eph. 5.9; Heb. 12.11; Jas. 3.18).

A happy exception to this neglect is the Marriage liturgy where, at least in the East, psalmody has not been ousted by hymns. After the betrothal with the exchange of rings, the Byzantine rite of crowning bride and groom begins with Psalm 128, whose pilgrim character reflects the couple's journey of love, growing together in fruitfulness. Their journey is symbolized as they are led in procession to the centre of the church with God's words of promise and joy ringing in their ears.

> Happy are all who fear the Lord.
> *Glory to you, our God, glory to you!*
> Those who walk in God's ways.
> *Glory to you, our God, glory to you!*
> You shall eat the fruit of your labours.
> *Glory to you, our God, glory to you!*
> You shall be happy and it shall be well with you.
> *Glory to you, our God, glory to you!*
> Your wife shall be as a fruitful vine
> within the walls of your home.
> *Glory to you, our God, glory to you!*

The bonding image of vine-branches bearing fruit in John 15 has long been part of the Methodist Covenant Service, where the congregation is rededicated to God. This often happens at the beginning of September, coinciding fortuitously with the completion of harvest. The fundamental sacrament of Christian discipleship, however, is baptism, and the Church of England has now brought a fuller range of psalms and readings into the liturgy of initiation.

> I will pour out my spirit upon your seed,
> and my blessing upon your offspring.
> They shall spring up as a green tamarisk,
> like willows beside channels of water . . .

> How high you lift my soul, O Lord,
> Anointed with fresh oil.
> The righteous like the palm bear fruit
> And grow like cedars tall.

Their roots are planted in your house,
  And, fresh with sap, mature,
At every age they still bear fruit
  To show the Lord is sure.

        Reading and Baptismal Gradual, Isaiah 44.3–4;
        Psalm 92.10–15 (Tunes: Amazing Grace, Rodmell)

In the northern Italy of fourth-century Ambrose we find an interesting ritual after the anointing and clothing of baptism. Candidates have their feet washed by the priest, recalling Jesus washing the disciples' feet at the Last Supper. Though this teaches the lesson of humility and service, Ambrose also sees the action as a sign of sanctification, so that where we touch the ground on which the snake of temptation was condemned to creep, our feet may take the holiness of God before us. The ritual was taken up in France and travelled to Ireland where we find it in the ninth-century Book of Stowe, accompanied by words from the psalms. The fourfold form suggests a commitment to the four gospels, especially as the fourth phrase echoes the fourth gospel's new commandment of love at the foot-washing.[17] Here we frame this Irish text with other verses that could be used when commissioning lay people for ministry.

There is one body and one Spirit, just as you have been called in the one hope of your calling: one Lord, one faith, one baptism. Make your way in the world worthy of your calling.

Those who are planted in the house of the Lord
shall flourish in the courts of our God.
They shall bear fruit and abound in fresh growth.

Jesus said, 'I am the Vine, you are the branches. Whoever abides in me and I in them bears much fruit.'

The Book of the Gospels is held open before those to be commissioned. They may be sprinkled with holy water as all say or sing

Alleluia, your Word is a lamp to my feet, O Lord.
Alleluia, come to my help and I shall be safe.
Alleluia, visit us with your salvation, O Lord.

Alleluia, you have handed on to us the commandment to have your heart of love: do not forsake the work of your hands.[18]

Sharing the story

The Word of God in worship affirms our common faith as well as our individual calling. For the marginalized, music has always been the voice of faith when other forms of public expression are forbidden, whether it be the spirituals of Afro-Caribbean slaves or the protest songs of black South Africans. Jewish experience has been an inspiration itself, challenging and overcoming oppression. Songs such as that of Miriam at the Exodus, Judith's hymn of victory or the chant of the exiles by the waters of Babylon, acknowledged even by their captors, encouraged the faith of the whole community.

The dialogue of cantor and congregation is a common way of encouraging one another. As well as the evidence of the psalms (46, 107, 136), Philo of Alexandria gives an insight into later Jewish usage in the contemplative community of the Therapeutai in Egypt. Their hymns were sometimes divided between choirs of men and women with everyone joining in a refrain, while on occasions such as vigils, the cantor might lead with the congregation responding in ritual dance.[19] The bonding experience of reciting prayer and promise from God's Word may still be seen in the *chevrah tehillim*, groups which arise outside formal synagogue worship simply to say the Psalter together. Christian apostles also advised their churches to 'let the word of Christ dwell among you in its richness, teaching and instructing each other with all wisdom in psalms, hymns and spiritual songs' (Col. 3.16; *cf.* Eph. 5.19). John Chrysostom encouraged his congregation to sing their antiphonal refrain to the psalm as a strengthening of their commitment to God:

> Do not think that you have come here only to say the words. You have come, so that, when you sing your part (*hupopsalleis*), you may consider that response to be a covenant. For when you sing '*As the hart longs for the water-springs, so longs my soul for you, O God*', you make a covenant

with God. For you have signed a contract without paper or ink; you have confessed with your voice that you love God more than all.[20]

The praise of worshippers may also be deepened by exploring the name of God as a musical mantra. The Psalmist seems to invite people 'to exult before God with (the chanting of) the name Yah' who is their glory and their music (Pss. 65.5; 118.14; cf. 105.3), suggesting a long, contemplative chant in the way in which Christian tradition later developed the Alleluia before the gospel with a lengthy melismatic jubilus on the last syllable 'Yah'.[21]

At the Daily Office it has long been the custom to invite the congregation to confirm their faith in the promises of God in a short responsory, a medium which is being increasingly explored in other services.

> My tongue shall tell the tale of your justice.
>   *When I sing to you, my lips shall rejoice.*
>   *Psalm 71.23–4* (Roman Divine Office)

The German Reformation developed other responses to the Word, especially in the cantata following the gospel. A study of Bach's work at St Thomas', Leipzig, has shown that he often drew upon psalm texts to affirm its message, sometimes from the proper of the Mass, now a resource regarded 'no longer as a fixed liturgical order but as an ordered, living proclamation of the Gospel'.[22] The good news of Christmas resounded with the response *'Our mouth be filled with laughter'* and the Gospel of the Ascension was celebrated with *'God has gone up with rejoicing'* (Pss. 126, 47 cf. BWV 110, 43). Here was a dynamic of liturgical constraint and liberty – with mandatory lessons but the freedom of the gospel in musical response and sermon. Worship leaders preparing preaching services might well follow the example of musicians like Bach and Schütz and quarry the psalms for their treasures.

Artists and musicians have taken up the language of psalmody to share comfort with a broken world. Celebrating the fiftieth anniversary of the capital Budapest in 1923, Kodály turned to the resilient faith of the Psalmist to speak to a newly independent but endangered nation, coping with thousands of refugees expelled by its neighbours.

> I would rather live in the wilderness,
> hide away in the wild forest,
> than live among those
> who do not let me speak the truth . . .
> You are just, O my Lord, in your judgment;
> the bloodsuckers in their time
> you do not bless them with good fortune,
> they shall not have a long time on earth.
> You uphold all the just, succour the pious, exalt the poor.

cf. *Psalm 55.7–8, 22–3*[23]

Against the ongoing ethnic conflicts of Europe the Taizé community prays for reconciliation, uniting pilgrims of all nations in song.

> *La ténèbre n'est point ténèbre devant toi;*
> *la nuit comme le jour est lumière.*

Psalm 139.12

The prophetic word sets our darkness before the light of God, where we are overcome neither by despair or complacency but transfigured by a vision destined to be shared with the world.

In Psalm 19, the personal companionship of God like the voice of a lover, as we saw earlier, comes together with this vision of universal truth, radiating like the sun and awesome as the silent music of the planets. But the words for creation telling and proclaiming God's glory (*sapar, nagad*) also appear when the Law is given to the people at Sinai, a story commemorated at Jewish Pentecost with this psalm. And we find Paul turning to his liturgical roots to depict the Church sharing the Gospel, which, like the Law, had first been revealed in the wind and fire of Pentecost (Rom. 10.18). In the Orthodox liturgy of that day, the sharing of the Psalmist's prophecy comes full circle. The voice of God recalled for the Hebrew musician the Law given at Sinai, resounding through creation yet dwelling intimately with the believer: now it becomes a hymn to celebrate the first Christian

preachers. For us, singing the same words, it is the voice of
prophets and saints, the voice of Mary who assented and gave
birth to the Word, the voice of the whole company of heaven
who encourage us to join our praises with theirs and let the
music of God's truth fill the world.

> *Through the prayers of her who bore God, O Saviour, save us.*
> The heavens are telling the glory of God,
>> the firmament gives the news of God's handiwork.
> Day to day pours forth the message,
>> and night to night makes knowledge news.
> There is no talk or words,
>> their voices are not heard.
> Into all the earth their sound went forth,
>> and their message to the ends of the world.
>> *Psalm 19 (Orthodox Antiphon for Pentecost)*

FOUR

Searching for Faith

God awaiting us

Every October the countdown to Christmas begins with crowds lured into stores, ready to spend vast amounts of money on presents that will 'make' Christmas. We search for familiar foods and for that unexpected present, the surprise that will recreate the magic of Christmas past. Beneath this orgy of commercialization lies a stifled spiritual desire to recover the mystery of something familiar yet new, known to us yet still to be explored. Something of this paradox is true about prayer.

> You are good, Lord, to the soul who seeks you, and what indeed to the one who comes upon you? . . . No one can seek you, if they have not already come upon you. You want yourself to be found, so that you may be sought; and you want to be sought that you may be found. You want to let us seek you and come upon you but not come upon you first. For, though we say, 'In the morning my prayer shall come before you' (Ps. 88.13), there is no doubt that every prayer is lukewarm to which your inspiration has not first come.[1]

We cannot hope to find what we seek unless we have some inkling of what we are looking for. The secret of prayer is discovering the God whose character is deep within us, waiting to be found.

From our baptism and before, we have been drawn, often unconsciously, to find God and only some distance along the

journey do we come to see this. For it is the very nature of God
to make the first move towards us. We hear God's archetypal cry
'Where are you, Adam?' repeated through the wanderings of the
wilderness and the protests of the prophets. God draws us into
friendship by various promptings over time: even apparently
sudden conversions are really a recognition of what God has been
doing all along. Pride in our own spiritual efforts may only
obscure God, as Simone Weil cautions:

> In the great images of mythology and folklore, in the par-
> ables of the gospel, it is God who seeks human beings . . .
> Human beings do not even take a step without being pushed
> or expressly called . . . To desire God and renounce all the
> rest, it is that alone that saves us.[2]

The coming of Christ is God's supreme initiative, inviting us
to return to our Maker. Gregory the Great sees this as a dance of
love, colourfully drawing on the picture of the lovers in the Song
of Songs and the psalm for Christmas Matins.

> Now you see the Truth, wanting us to run after her; she
> was manifested in the flesh and danced for us. She danced
> for joy like a giant running the course, so that we might say
> to her from our hearts: 'Take us with you; let us run after
> the fragrance of your perfumed oils!'
> cf. *Psalm 19.5; Song of Songs 1.4*[3]

Prayer is the dialogue between God and human beings,
expressed in liturgy with the frequent use of responses when we
call for God to answer or God seeks our response. But before
we can presume to pray at all, we have to realize that we are
dependent on God, as the beginning of the Daily Office recalls:

> O Lord, open thou our lips:
> And our mouth shall shew forth thy praise.
> *Psalm 51.15* (Book of Common Prayer)

Commenting on this verse, John Donne remarks that we only
respond at all because God assists us: 'all . . . consummations,
beginnings and perfectings are of God, of God alone; but in the
way there is a concurrence on our part (by a successive continu-

ation of God's grace) in which God proceeds as a Helper.'[4] Part of that grace is that God gives us words to match our quest. 'What shall I say? . . . Where shall I seek him? . . . Whom shall I ask?' Anselm asks questions in his prayers that we know well but the answer comes in an unconscious outpouring of reassurance drawn from years of reciting the Psalter:

> The joy of my heart fails me;
> my laughter is turned to mourning . . .
> but God is the strength of my heart and my portion for
>   ever . . .
> to you my heart has said, Seek my face;
> your face, Lord, I have sought . . .
>
> *Psalms 73.26; 27.8—9*[5]

Scripture thus becomes a means of grace because it gives us a language, even a language of doubt, with which we can speak to God whose voice it also carries.

Silence

Even before we come to words, body and mind need to be prepared for our meeting with God. The solemn Jewish 'Amidah or Standing Prayer, introduced by the invitation 'Lord, open my lips', has sometimes been marked by congregants physically stepping forward at the beginning as if entering the presence of God. Syrian Orthodox Christians approach worship by prostrating themselves on the ground. For the Psalmist, it is natural that our first approach to God should be silence.

> My soul is all silence, waiting on God alone,
>   from whom comes my salvation . . .
> O my soul, wait in silence for God alone,
>   from whom comes all my hope.
>
> *Psalm 62.1, 5*

The focus for our meaningful connection with God is not the prayer itself but the 'pray-er'.

And, as for me, I am a prayer before you, God,
   at the proper time.

Psalm 69.13[6]

The stillness of body and the attentiveness of the mind makes us a precious offering of love to God. Our inactivity and devotion recognizes that God is all in all for us.

> Your mind will be swallowed up in awestruck wonder, your senses will be silent . . . your tongue unable to speak, and your heart incapable of praying; for in wonder at these divine acts even prayer becomes inactive . . . Even our bones in their silence will offer up praise to God during this apparent inactivity, as the prophet says, 'All my bones shall say "O Lord, who is like you?"'[7]

In the silence we are aware that we come before the one who holds the key to our life, one who alone can make us the person we were intended to be. Zephaniah's promise that the Lord 'will be silent in love' (3.17) is interpreted by some Jewish commentators as meaning that God's love covers our sins with a gracious silence, removing our awkwardness and unworthiness. The unspeakable nature of this grace in the incarnation of Christ is described by Ignatius of Antioch as 'God's eternal Word proceeding from silence.'[8] Prayer begins with the silence which, for the prophets, was a sign that God is about to act (Hab. 2.20; Zech. 2.13). We may come with feelings of guilt or anxiety but we know that God is ready to love us and repair our brokenness. Writing of the penitent coming to make their confession, Kierkegaard says that 'the stillness also impresses them, yet not in the melancholy mood of misunderstanding, but rather with the seriousness of eternity'.[9]

My own experience of celebrating Mass each week with a community of people with learning disabilities has taught me how those who are less verbally dependent often have an instinct for silence which is more perceptive than many congregations. For most of us this has to be learnt. Just as psalmody was the staple diet of monastic life from the beginning, its evocative spirituality is still inspiring communities who seek to explore meditation though silence and music. This is a tall order to fulfil in places like Taizé and Iona, constantly invaded by thousands of pilgrims, each bringing their own needs and hopes as well as differing cultures. But the enduring strength of this sung prayer is also the strength of psalmody: it puts us in touch with our own individual emotions and gives us space to express them but in a form that draws us together as one soul before God. When Scripture is sung, we are also able to find layer upon layer of meaning and many resonances with other parts of the Bible. As these songs deepen our experience, the international context broadens it and the use of other languages in worship becomes not a barrier but a release into a less verbally conscious form of prayer.

> *Notre âme attend le Seigneur.*
> *En lui la joie de notre coeur.*
>
> Psalm 33.20–1 (Taizé)

> I waited, I waited on the Lord . . .
> He bent down low and remembered me,
> when he heard my prayer.
>
> Psalm 40.1 (Iona)

In parish worship silence is often used to give time for private intercession or reflection rather than contemplation.

> In the Penitential Act and after the invitation to pray the Collect the people should turn their thoughts to themselves; after the readings and the homily they should meditate briefly on what they have heard; after the Communion they should praise and pray to God in their hearts.[10]

These exercises may be valuable individually and corporately but there is a danger of having an agenda to pray through, which may or may not bring us closer to God.

Significantly, the more contemplative element in the instructions on the *Roman Missal* is associated with the period after communion, nurtured in the Catholic tradition by other times of corporate devotion before the Blessed Sacrament. Some Anglicans sustain a similarly intense silence before early morning Mass where their prayer to be one with Christ is quickened by fasting.

At such moments God is revealed to us as a gift of love in the silence. The 'silent waiting' of the Quaker meeting has been compared to this liturgical moment: 'Inwardly the Divine Leader of worship . . . may in the silence bring an inward climax which is as definite as the climax of the Mass when the host is elevated in adoration.'[11] Silence after the Eucharistic Prayer is common to most rites as we cross the threshold between thanksgiving and communion but silence can, as in Quaker meetings, be the medium of disclosure itself, expressing the apophatic mystery of God. R. S. Thomas sensed the way that words may actually obstruct our knowledge of God in prayer.

> Prompt me, God;
> But not yet. When I speak
> Though it be you who speak
> Through me, something is lost.
> The meaning is in the waiting.
>
> *'Kneeling'*

Arguing with God

Like any relationship, this dialogue is not without its tensions; and the value of the psalms is that they have no pietistic inhibitions about voicing anger towards God when prayers go unanswered and God no longer seems to care. Then we feel that God has abandoned us in our need, leaving an empty silence to taunt us in our prayers. We feel forgotten by a God from whom we seem to be separated by an endless void (*cf.* Pss. 10, 13, 22, 28, 35, 44, 83, 109).

> How long, O Lord? Will you forget me for ever?
> How long will you hide your face from me?
> How long must I be abandoned to my own devices,
>   with sorrow in my heart all the day long?
> How long shall my enemy triumph over me?
>
> *Psalm 13.1–2*

Yet, as Jesus suggests in his parables of persistence – the widow seeking justice and the friend disturbing a sleeping house-

hold to find food – the uncomfortable silence of (as yet) unanswered prayer is part of our wrestling with God for a just outcome to
our distress. The God who answers too readily may turn out
to be just another mirage like the seductive certainties of funda-
mentalism. Only in the silence can we hear the voice of God,
which, as in the incarnation, may be a weak and vulnerable cry:

> God, though to Thee our psalm we raise
> No answering voice comes through the skies;
> To Thee the trembling sinner prays
> But no forgiving voice replies;
> Our prayer seems lost in desert ways,
> Our hymn in the vast silence dies . . .
>
> And Thou art silent, whilst Thy world
> Contends about its many creeds
> And hoists confront with flags unfurled
> And zeal is flushed and pity bleeds
> And truth is heard, with tears impearled,
> A moaning voice among the reeds.
>
> *'Nondum' (Gerard Manley Hopkins)*

The darker side of the spiritual life is there in the prayers of
Jesus, who turned to the psalms to voice his own feelings
of emptiness and struggle and to question why God had abandoned him (John 12.27 – Ps. 42.6; Matt. 26.38 – Ps. 42.5; John
19.28 – Ps. 42.2; Mark 15.34 – Ps. 22.1). This tradition gave
him permission to question, as it gives us permission too, but we
should not regard this as extraordinary. As the gospels show,
questioning has been a fundamental means of teaching and
learning in rabbinical Judaism and is vital to faith itself. When we
question, we are facing reality and coming to terms with where
we stand. We are no longer helpless victims, but people who are
trying to put faith into practice and be free of all that oppresses
us. And our questioning leads us away from vindictiveness to the
God who vindicates all who suffer unjustly, not only us. We are
drawn out of the chaos of the despair that overwhelms us towards
God's universal justice. So it is that alongside the Psalmist's
question, we begin to find faith confirmed:

When I call, answer me, O God of justice;
from anguish you released me, have mercy and hear me!
> *Psalm 4.1 (Night Prayer, Roman Divine Office)*

But faith may not come. The pain may be too great to believe in God.

For your sake we are being killed all day long:
and counted as sheep for slaughter.
Rouse yourself! Why are you asleep, Lord?
Wake up, and do not abandon us for ever.
> *Psalm 44.22–3*

Few texts have had such an influence on Jewish writing, especially in the poetry and memoirs of the Holocaust. Around these words a whole theology was developed, hallowing martyrdom for God. Like the Psalmist, however, others have felt unconvinced that any God worth worshipping could want such a sacrifice; they have come to reject the warrior God who intervenes and any idea that God is a special shepherd to a flock which is seen to have been wiped out.[12] Psalm 44 itself does not go beyond the angry cry for help, but it gives us words for a time of such pain and refuses to let us be passive victims. In this we may find God is very much awake, though not the God we had imagined, for the psalms can be radically subversive of other biblical images of God. Waiting on God is not passive acceptance of what we have been told.

Urgency, therefore, always has some place in our daily prayer, if not for ourselves, then for others, quite apart from our longing to be with God. So the Daily Office begins with verses which have been sung since the time of Benedict and probably long before:

O God, come to our aid:
O Lord, make haste to help us.
> (Roman Divine Office)

O God, make speed to save us:
O Lord, make haste to help us.
> *Psalm 70.1 (Common Worship)*

The parallelism of the psalms, often in the form of question and answer, intensifies the urgency of the quest. It is a technique we find in the dialogue of lovers in the Song of Songs, in the liturgical drama of the Passion Gospel and Reproaches, and was consummately developed by Bach in his use of the double chorus in the St Matthew Passion, questioning and answering each other from either end of the church:

Come, you daughters, help me lament, see –	*Who?*
the bridegroom, see him	*How?*
as a lamb . . . see	*What?*
his patience.	*Why?*
for our guilt.	

Persistence in prayer became a particular theme in Advent liturgy. Inspired by the words of Psalm 80: *Excita potentiam tuam et veni* ('Stir up your stength and come'), the Roman rite sustained this cry throughout the mass texts of the season. Though they were more penitential than intercessory, it is a pity that this urgent call to God did not survive liturgical reform. 'Stir up' remains in the collects of the *Book of Common Prayer* and in an Advent collect for *Common Worship*, taken from the *Gelasian Sacramentary*.

> O Lord, raise up, we pray, your power and come among us, and with great might succour us; that, whereas, through our sins and wickedness we are grievously hindered in running the race that is set before us, your bountiful grace and mercy may speedily help and deliver us . . .

The encouragement of the psalms for us to be honest about our impatience with God is an important corrective for Christians who often equate forgiveness with submissiveness. Such a 'doormat' spirituality only succeeds in repressing deep needs and creating an unreal relationship with what is a false projection of God. Openness, however, awakens us from the introverted anger of depression to a more positive search for justice and right relationships in our lives.

Keeping watch

For the Psalmist the individual's quest for God belonged within the whole worshipping community. The dialogic structure of lament and oracle shows how prophetically gifted ministers offered the people's intercessions in the Temple and declared God's response. These psalms lend themselves to sustained prayer in our own worship at vigils for example. Their focus on God's faithful love and maternal compassion and their commitment to justice complements the feminist insight into waiting as 'a tool charged with hope', as Mary Grey describes it.

> It is one way which women's spirituality offers of bridging the gap between being and doing. It is the one activity in which women have been engaged from time immemorial – waiting at the sick-bed of a child, waiting with the dying, keeping vigil with the dead, standing outside embassies pleading for the missing . . .[13]

The power of such intercession is its personal commitment to a community, not as an ideological concept but as a real body of people who know they belong to each other.

This is a role which women have always fulfilled in the Church, and the lives of the mystics bear witness to the cost of this intervention as they placed themselves in the vulnerable no man's land between the needy and their enemies. Hildegard of Bingen chose to have her community read rather than sing the office, a considerable punishment for a musician but one she was ready to endure in order to defend the right of burial for someone who was wrongly supposed to be a heretic. One of the best documented ministries of intercession is the life of the Norfolk mystic Margery Kempe, who was commended by Julian of Norwich herself for her tears of compassion. Priests came to her to ask for her prayers for the dying and she exercised a continuing ministry among the elderly, the lepers and with other women who suffered from depression. On one occasion at Mass she had a premonition of a disaster and cried out

> 'Alas, dear and worthy Lord, what shall I do for the people?' She was given an affirmation which many of us

need in our intercessory prayer, 'It is enough for you to do as you do', and she concluded: 'Show your mercy and your goodness upon them, help them, send them true contrition, and let them never die in their sin.'[14]

These words from Psalm 85 have often been used in intercession. We find them, for example, in a 'Vigil for prisoners and those who sit in darkness', where they are placed between Isaiah's promise that God will remember the suffering and a message of peace and reconciliation in the Christ who breaks down every wall of separation:

You have been kind, O Lord, to your land:
    you overturned the imprisonment of Jacob.
You forgave the guilt of your people:
    you covered all their sin.
You put away all your displeasure once before:
    and turned from your bitter rage . . .
Will you not turn us back and make us live again:
    that your people may find joy in you?
Show us your mercy, O Lord:
    and grant us your salvation.

The feeling of being victimized and punished by God does not offer us a sound theology of what God is like but the Psalmist gives us the words to say what we really feel and guides us through those emotions, clouded by failure and anxiety, to see life in the perspective of God's mercy. As one medieval preacher prayed, 'Show us your mercy, for we are not yet capable of seeing your glory.'[15]

The prophetic intercession of psalmody has become rooted in the liturgy of the Church. For hundreds of years Anglicans have prayed this verse in the Daily Office: 'O Lord, shew thy mercy upon us: And grant us thy salvation.' Roman Catholics seek forgiveness at mass with the words, 'Lord, show us your mercy and love. And grant us your salvation.' This petition is already found in a seventh-century Irish Office for the Sick but the English use is attested in the thirteenth century 'Bidding of the Bedes', an interesting form of intercession in the vernacular which developed in the Sarum rite, using verses from the psalms. In Jerusalem and probably Rome, evening prayer had ended with a series of biddings with the Kyrie response but in Celtic countries, as we see first in the sixth-century Office of Columbanus, these were replaced by a series of *capitella*, petitionary verses preceded by biddings covering a wide range of needs.[16] We find a parallel use of psalmody at the end of Vespers in the Spanish Mozarabic rite, possibly originating as a stational chant for a procession to the baptistery or a chapel of martyr's relics.[17] The texts often stress the joy and cost of discipleship: the verses on Palm Sunday actually change the psalm, apparently to pray for those to be baptized at Easter:

> Teach them, Lord, the way of your statutes . . .
> Grant them understanding, Lord . . .
>
> *Psalm 119.33–4*

These petitions make us ask whether our liturgy has become too introverted, too addicted to a kind of pastoral valium, to allow the prophetic voice to be heard. In the Syrian Church Ephrem was inspired by Daniel's description of angelic beings as 'watchers' (*'ire*) to see Christ as the Wakeful One coming at his nativity to call us to a life of watchfulness:

> The Wakers rejoice today
>   for the Wakeful One has come to wake us up:
> on this night who shall sleep
>   when all creation is awake?[18]

Keeping watch, however, is not a popular practice in liturgy or life. Christopher Moody has given a timely warning that 'the modern pressure always to be busy and "pastorally active" has obscured any image which carries with it the passive connotations of waiting for something to happen or watching while others work'. The drive to equip clergy with management skills can lead to an obsessive concern for planning and correct structures while vision and discernment are lost. He highlights the important communal task of discernment which is often 'a case of the minister attending to voices that were already present, especially those which cause discomfort and unease'.[19]

Just such a voice is heard by the prophetic minister in Psalm 80, who puts into words the anger and desperation of the community:

> O Lord God of hosts,
> how long will you be angry at your people's prayer?
> You feed them with the bread of tears;
> you give them abundance of tears to drink.
> You have made us the derision of our neighbours,
> and our enemies laugh us to scorn.
> *Advent Gradual* (Common Worship)

The cry 'How long?', echoed by generations of suffering, brings the injustice and protest to God with a force that makes our average intercessions look rather bland. To be watchful, as Jesus asked of his friends in Gethsemane, means sharing people's discomforting doubts and having the courage to pray them publicly.

A journey of hope

Watching in prayer is not some neurosis that preys on the anxious but the courage to journey into the cloud of unknowing, trusting the God who leads us. The traditional introit for Advent Sunday sets this hope before us and the psalm's Hebrew structure – with each verse beginning with the next letter of the alphabet – gives momentum to the path of prayer.

> To you, O Lord, I lift up my soul;
>   O my God, in you I trust . . .
> Make me to know your ways, O Lord,
>   and teach me your paths.
> Lead me in your truth and teach me,
> for you are the God of my salvation;
>   for you have I hoped all the day long.
> *Psalm 25.1, 4–5* (Common Worship)

The one who guides us is like a parent on whose faithful love (*ḥesedh*) we may utterly depend. In the Psalter God's faithfulness and maternal commitment (*raḥmim* – compassion from the womb) constantly mirror and interpret each other (Pss. 40.11;

51.1; 69.16; 77.8–9; 103.4; 106.45–6; 119.76–7). We put our faith and therefore our hope in the love which has been there from the beginning, continually forgiving and accepting.

> Remember, Lord, your compassion and love.
> for they are from everlasting.
> Remember not the sins of my youth or my transgressions,
> but think on me in your goodness, O Lord,
>   according to your steadfast love.
>
> *Psalm 25.6–7*

The reliability of God's love gives us the basis on which to form our own relationships for 'God by satisfying my self-love hath enabled and encouraged me to love others.'[20]

The endurance of those who hold on to hope 'all the day long' becomes a strength to others, especially when they see faith in people who seem most vulnerable. The Hebrew verb *kawah*, variously translated 'to wait' or 'to hope', carries the underlying image of thread which is twisted or stretched, thin and taut but strong. Samson Raphael Hirsch describes those who hope in God as feeling 'drawn to the Lord with every fibre of their being'.[21] The total commitment of whatever fragile thread of faith we have is its very strength.

The experience of God's past grace and present help gradually reveals a new horizon. That perspective must always remain partly unknown and the temptation to fill it with our own ideals or wants can only blind our vision of God. Hope cannot be placed in God just in case our plans do not work out even if we have to face the agnosticism which is an inevitable part of faith. Eliot claimed that, in contrast to the certainty of Marxists, his own beliefs were held with a scepticism which he never hoped to lose.[22] Hope for the Psalmist is a quest of God's making. Anything else is a kind of ambition circumscribed by our limited horizons.

>   I'll not reproach
> The road that winds, my feet that err.
>   Access, Approach
> Art Thou, Time, Way, and Wayfarer.
>
> *'I am the Way' (Alice Meynell)*

We come to recognize that the detours and failures on the way
are essential if we are to arrive at the destination, for they change
us and make us ready to receive God's gift. 'One simply cannot
be today what God will form tomorrow', as one liturgist has
written.[23]

Psalm 25 sets before us not the frantic preparations of Advent
for Christmas but a horizon of justice and compassion beyond
our imagination:

> The Lord is good and upright,
> showing the path to those who stray,
> guiding the humble in the right path,
> and teaching the way to the poor.
> God's ways are steadfastness and truth
> for those faithful to the covenant decrees.
>
> *Psalm 25.8–10 (Advent Gradual*, Roman Missal)

The Psalmist knows that this journey of hope cannot be under-
taken without clearing our path of guilt, both for wilful acts
of rebellion and missed opportunities. Jonathan Magonet has
suggested that beneath the controlled alphabetic order of this
psalm lies a deep emotional and religious crisis.[24] The fear of
shame expressed at the beginning and the end implies that
without forgiveness the future is a closed door. The sinner is
hanging on by a thin thread of hope but we are encouraged to
believe that our waiting will not be in vain.

The prayer of repentance never becomes so introspective that
all else is forgotten. Indeed, it is very much the cry of a Covenant
people asking that God vindicate integrity and guide a nation
under attack. Yet there is an awareness that we cannot pray for
God's liberation to be revealed if it is not revealed in us. Prayer
cannot be limited to answers to immediate needs or just
demands: God's goal for us lies on the long road of faith and right
conduct.

> Look upon my adversity and misery: and forgive me all
>   my sin.
> Consider mine enemies, how many they are:
>   and they bear tyrannous hate against me.

O keep my soul, and deliver me:
    let me not be confounded, for I have put my trust in
      thee.
Let perfectness and righteous dealing wait upon me:
    for my hope hath been in thee.
Deliver Israel, O God: out of all his troubles.
                    Psalm 25.18–22 (Book of Common Prayer)

A cloud of light

We may remain agnostic about finding an answer to suffering
but, when we share in the intercession of a community, we have
no right to become apathetic about it. Our human need to search
for some light which gives meaning to sorrow is revealed in the
prayers for light which have found their way into intercessions at
the close of the Daily Office. Since at least the eighth century,
Christians have wanted to pray 'Lighten our darkness' as night
falls. In the fragile hours before dawn Syrian Orthodox conclude
their Morning Prayer with a prayer for light to eyes and heart,
whose name (*bo'uto* – supplication) suggests its intercessory
origin.

> Shine forth upon us, our Lord,
> and from your light we shall shine like the day . . .
> With the day, may your light enlighten our thoughts
> and remove from our minds the darkness of error.
> Now the creation is all light, give light also to our
> hearts . . .
>
>   *Kurisumala Ashram*

During seasons of expectation such as Advent the search for
revelation takes the dialogue of responses and transforms it into a
more dramatic form. The structure of psalmody with its question
and answer is well suited to express the prophetic tension of our
doubts and hopes, encouraging us not to settle for anything less
than an answer which is of God. We can only ask too little of
God, never too much. The medieval Matin Responsory for
Advent Sunday draws on these rich resources to arouse our

expectation of the God who guides us, whoever and wherever
we are, with the power of one who cares for us.

R   I look from afar,
and now I see the power of God coming,
and a cloud covering the whole earth.
    Go out to meet him and say,
Tell us, are you the One who is coming to reign
    amongst your people Israel?
V   All you dwellers upon earth, high and low,
rich and poor as one together.
    Go out to meet him and say . . .
V   Hear us, you that shepherd Israel,
leading Joseph like a sheep.
    Tell us, are you the One who is coming to reign
    amongst your people Israel?
V   Lift up your heads, O gates,
be lifted high, you everlasting gates.
and he shall enter,
the King of glory, who is to reign
amongst your people Israel. *Gloria and R*
    Matthew 11.3: Psalms 49.1–2: 80.1; 24.7

The journey is in the company of others. We are not alone,
but part of God's flock, whatever our race or wealth.

The bringing together of personal expectation and hope for
the world is shown in the ever popular Christingle Service,
originating in the Moravian Church in 1747, which continues to
hold it before Christmas in a mood of anticipation. Neil Alexander recalls his childhood memories of freshly baked buns, the
scent of beeswax and aroma of coffee, reflecting that the most
telling thing about these symbols in the Moravian community is
the sense of belonging.[25] We may sometimes have to keep watch
on our own but we are always part of the people of God who
unfailingly comes to keep our promised tryst in worship. As long
as we belong to God and each other, we are the living proof that
God belongs to those in darkness and need and they will not lack
others to watch and pray for them. It is for each other that we
carry the light.

The Psalmist asks us to expect that light to dawn on us in worship. We come, unable to understand God's ways as we see the arrogant and violent prosper in the world: only when 'I enter the holy places of God, then I learn to look for their end' (Ps. 73.17). The plural suggests our own spiritual path of understanding as we journey from one revelation of God to a deeper one.[26] In the liturgy we see even evil in a new perspective, as we continue constant in prayer for the light of God to overcome the dark.

> Hear, O Shepherd, hear us, for you lead us like your flock,
> from your throne of angels, shine forth.
> Stir up your strength and come to save us.
>
> R   *O God, bring us home;*
>   *show us the light of your face*
>   *and we shall be safe.*
>
> Let your hand bless your chosen son,
> the one you made so strong for yourself.   R
> Then we will not turn back from you;
> give us life again
> and we will tell the wonders of your name.   R
>
>   *Psalm 80.1–3, 17–19* (Christingle Prayers for
>   Children in Danger)

FIVE

Love Rediscovered

First love

> I would not have anyone think that I became a catholic
> because I was convinced of the truth, though I was con-
> vinced of the truth. I became a catholic because I fell in love
> with the truth. And love is an experience. I saw. I heard. I
> felt. I tasted. I touched. And that is what lovers do.[1]

This confession from the artist Eric Gill about his conversion
is the secret of faith. We cannot be threatened or indoctrinated
into real faith. We must first be drawn by the love of God
attracting us before we can learn to see sin in proper perspective.
To know our failure and explore our guilt without being held by
love is to walk into hell. Some spiritual directors actually warn
people not to force themselves to speak about things which
have been unmentionable. Sharing them with the wrong person,
however professional, may only do further damage to mind and
spirit. According to Julian of Norwich, God knows well the
dangers of repentance without feeling loved, 'for our sin is so
vile and so horrible that our Lord out of courtesy will not show
it to us except in the light of God's grace and mercy'.[2]

Grace must come before sin can be confessed but Christians
are not always good at affirming God's love for themselves or
anyone else. The Church, by its nature and calling, attracts
people who are aware of their own insecurity, lovelessness and
failure. Though religion should be a way to work through these
experiences, insecurity may opt for a safer, rigid discipline of

worship and behaviour which represses difficulties and drives us
to repress others whose openness threatens us.

More than any other, Psalm 5 1 has come to express our need
of forgiveness and it begins with the love of God, expressed
in that combination of enduring faithfulness (*ḥesedh*) and the
compassion that wells up from a mother's womb (*raḥmim*).

> Have mercy on me, O God,
> according to your faithful love:
> according to the abundance of your mother-love,
> blot out my transgressions.
>
> *Psalm 5 1 . 1*

Here is the lasting commitment of a caring parent who cannot
stop loving, for 'none can forfeit this relationship because even
the most degenerate among human beings still remains God's
child'.[3] The same conviction journeys with us in Anglican
services during Lent in the oft-repeated words of the Collect for
Ash Wednesday: 'Almighty and everlasting God, you hate
nothing that you have made.'

Love is the antidote to the disintegration of our personality. If
we see ourselves and our sins only in our own light or in the
opinion of the friends we choose to agree with us, we have
chosen the road to self-despair. The danger of some versions of
Christian religion as well as some New Age cults is that they
choose from a menu of their own devising, and fail to encounter
reality through the love of the Other. The philosopher Martin
Buber understood that we only discover our own identity in our
friendship and conversation with God, for 'all real living is
meeting'. The believer is free to grow in their knowledge of
truth because they have not imposed their own conditions. 'The
self-willed person does not believe and does not meet. They do
not know any solidarity, but only the feverish world outside and
a feverish desire to use it.'[4] The Russian theologian Pavel Florensky also explored this encounter with God, observing that love
is not just desire but giving and receiving: people cannot be
possessed; they remain the person they are. Authentic love will
always affirm the other's identity in a relationship of interdependence, yet in the perception of the other person we find a

truth about ourselves that otherwise would remain unkown. 'A friend', Florensky explains, 'is not only an "I" but *another* "I", *another* for "I".* Friendship becomes the contemplation of oneself through the friend in God.' With such support and insight we may face deprivation of home or wealth for John Chrysostom tells us, whoever has a friend 'has another self'.[5]

Cleansing

Confession of our sin has, therefore, to be expressed in a realm such as worship where God's love is kept before our eyes and our solidarity strengthens one another. The title of Psalm 51 suggests that it is David's confession of adultery, which we might imagine to be a private prayer, but his fasting and penitence were public acts and the psalm is a proclamation to others of God's readiness to forgive. Confession can never be set apart from the people of God to whom we belong. At Yom Kippur, the great Jewish holy day of fasting and confession, the forms of penitence are in the plural although the services encourage profound personal examination. The medieval Spanish poet, Solomon Ibn Gabirol, brings corporate and personal together in a poem of preparation inspired by this psalm.

> O God, You are my God!
> I seek You early, where Your chosen ones gather to pray.
> I tell of Your faithfulness, I speak of Your greatness.
> When I cry, answer me,
> on this day when I stand in Your congregation.
> 'Lord, open my lips and my mouth shall declare Your
>   praise.'
>
> . . . When I cry, answer me,
> on this day when the cords of sin that hold me are broken.
> 'Wash me clean from my iniquity and purify me from my
>   sin.'
>
> (FPJW)

Preparing for praise by reflecting on grace is also a hallmark of Christian liturgy and the Psalmist's sense of God's overwhelming love may explain why, from the fourth century, Psalm 51 is consistently sung at the people's Office of Matins, celebrating the recreation which God brings afresh every morning. We catch a feeling of corporate renewal as we hear Basil describe his congregation at Caesarea. 'After passing the night with a variety of psalmody interspersed with our prayers, once the day is dawning, all of us in common, as with one voice and one heart, raise the psalm of confession to the Lord, each one making their own the words of repentance.'[6]

In the service of penitence the psalmist's prayer could be put to more radical use. The *Gelasian Sacramentary* tells how the seventh-century Church of Rome received penitents back into the fold before mass on Maundy Thursday. The deacon would present each person as they prostrated themselves before the bishop and intercede on their behalf:

> Therefore, moved by such examples to an act of penance,
> this penitent, in the sight of a grieving church,
> implores you, reverend Bishop, and says,
> *'I acknowledge my iniquities and my sin is ever before me.'*[7]

From this public reception of reconciled sinners the psalm found its way into the confession used for individual penitents, who are supported by a sense of solidarity in some Anglican and Lutheran rites with the priest and penitent saying the psalm together. In a more corporate setting, these words form part of the Methodist Covenant Service where the congregation makes their own confession in silence and then joins in common prayer.

> Have mercy on me, O God,
> in your constant love;
> in the fullness of your mercy
> blot out my offences.
> Wash away all my guilt,
> and cleanse me from my sin.

In Wesley's day this service concluded a period when the local church was helped to examine itself before God. We rightly regard preparation as essential before an individual makes their confession yet happily expect spontaneous repentance from a congregation, most of whom will not have privately prepared for communion, led by a priest whose sacristry is a frenzied centre of parish administration just before mass. The health of the church is better served by fewer confessions of sin and more opportunity to reflect and resolve to amend our ways.

Ash Wednesday is such an occasion. Before the grace of God we come face to face with the one who searches our hearts and leads us to see the truth about our sin in the charred remains of our palms, hosannas and promises eagerly made, now in ashes.

> Against you only have I sinned
> and done what is evil in your sight,
> So that you are justified in your sentence
> and righteous in your judgment.
> I have been wicked even from my birth,
> a sinner when my mother conceived me.
> Behold, you desire truth deep within me
> and shall make me understand wisdom in the depths
> of my heart.
>
> *Psalm 51.4–6* (Common Worship)

This implies neither original sin nor illegitimacy. Rather, the Hebrew word 'conceived' (*yehmathni*) suggests the inner core of our human identity which is surrounded and nurtured by the warm but fallible body of the mother. The God who made us so vulnerable should look upon us with compassion and teach our inner spiritual nature how to channel our physical energies.

Despite this compassion, indeed because of it, each of us has to acknowledge our own guilt. Our task is not to list other people's sins and excuse ours by comparison but to know ourselves. In the Eighteen Benedictions of the Jewish liturgy, after the three opening prayers of praise, the first petition is for understanding and the second for repentance. God's grace gives us the maturity to know ourselves and the dignity to answer for our own actions. For the healing of the sinner, this recognition of the truth has to be audible; Maimonides, for example, insisted that the confession of sin at Yom Kippur must be recited, not silent.[8] God has no need to be informed of what is known to the

One who sees all but 'the words serve both to connect the confessor with God the listener and to keep the two at a distance from each other.'⁹ Distance gives us the objectivity to see the greatness of the sins we have dismissed and the pettiness of some guilt which obsesses us.

And there is the distance we have created by sin. For sin is the assertion of my independence from all other considerations. It is the belief that I alone count. We exchange the loving purposes of God for a captivity to selfish moods and ambition over which we no longer have any control. An open acknowledgment of sin makes us aware of the Other waiting for us in love. The situation is beautifully portrayed in a medieval prayer, attributed to Hildegard, on Christ with the woman taken in adultery. The accusing crowd has departed and 'these two remained, the wretched heart and the tender heart'.¹⁰ In the love of the Other we know not only our sins but rediscover ourselves. The knowledge of such love, however, has to be shown, contact made, for that distance to be bridged. The Psalmist looks to the ritual of purging with hyssop, often used for sprinkling sacrificial blood and washing with water, remedies for contact with disease or death (*cf.* Lev. 14.1; Num. 19.6). Some act of cleansing may well have accompanied the psalm, for even under the restrictions of exile, Ezekiel was offended by ritual uncleanness and uses similar sacrificial imagery to speak of the Lord sprinkling clean water upon the people (Ezek. 4.13–14; 22.26; 36.25).

Christian liturgists have often quarried these texts for baptism and have pointed to the place of ritual cleansing in the Jewish Qumran community as an important background for the work of John the Baptist. But there are other aspects, more theological than historical, which may broaden our understanding. Karen Pusey suggests that Qumran may have instituted an initial purification of the flesh to be followed by a final purification of the spirit, and she cites Jewish scholars who link both proselyte baptism and the Holy Spirit with the Shekinah, the glory of God's presence, under whose protective wings initiates would come.¹¹ Certainly water and the Spirit imply something yet to be fulfilled, both in the account of creation, in the prophet's promise to the exiles, and in the Psalmist's prayer to be cleansed and guided by the Holy Spirit. In the Coptic rite of baptism our prayer and God's pledge are brought together as the priest mixes the oil of chrism and water in the font, singing on behalf of the candidate, 'Make a holy heart within me, O God; renew a right spirit within me, Alleluia!' When the truth and promise of baptism are joyfully remembered, the sacrament renews its power and we know ourselves forgiven and kept in God's grace for ever. The 'Asperges' of the Roman Mass is an example of how our baptism prophetically demonstrates God's forgiveness here and now, while looking to our hope in eternity.

> O purify me, then I shall be clean;
> O wash me, I shall be whiter than snow.
> Have mercy on me, God, in your kindness.

After the sprinking of water, the priest prays:
> May almighty God cleanse us of our sins,
> and through the eucharist we celebrate
> make us worthy to sit at his table
> in his heavenly kingdom. Amen.

cf. *Psalm 51.7, 1*

Healing

Cleansing may also be a channel of healing both to the individual and the community. Indians of North America still purify themselves by washing their faces with sweet grass herb before dancing in those gatherings whose name (*pau wau*) indicates their origin as the dances of medicine men. The Church of Southern Africa brings purification and healing together in its ministry to the sick, but carefully avoids making a link between sin and sickness which may not be valid.

The minister may sprinkle the sick person and the room with holy water, saying,
> Purge me with hyssop, and I shall be clean:
> wash me, and I shall be whiter than snow.

The minister prays with the sick person . . .
> Almighty God, giver of life and health, grant healing to N,

that rejoicing in your love he may be made whole and live
to your glory; through Jesus Christ our Lord. Amen.

Other people may be invited to lay hands on the sick person.

Ritual cleansing and renewal bring the joy of being part of the
community again. Having been isolated physically and spiritually
from the congregation and its liturgy, we need to feel
incorporated in that body again.

> Let me hear joy and gladness:
> let the bones that you have crushed rejoice.
>
> *Psalm 51.8*

The joy of being accepted despite our weaknesses explains
why penitential prayers are often set to music of great beauty.
The plainsong *Kyrie* of the *Missa de Angelis*, Allegri's setting of this
Miserere psalm, Fauré's *Requiem* or the Negro spiritual – all thrill
us with a poignant delight. The theme is taken up in the story of
the eighteenth-century Polish Hassidic leader, Baal Shem Tov.
Coming upon a city just before New Year, he asked about the
way the Rabbi led the service on solemn days. 'He weds all
the confessions of Yom Kippur to joyful melodies', he was told.
He sent for the Rabbi and asked him, 'Why do you recite the
confession so joyfully?' The Rabbi replied, 'When a royal slave
removes unsightly things from his master's courtyard, he is happy
because he has done it out of love for him. Likewise, I rejoice
when I remove objectionable things from my heart, for thereby I
give pleasure to the King of kings.'[12] Jesus also told of the angels'
joy in heaven when a sinner repents. The joy of forgiveness
springs from restored communion with God and with each other
and there can be no doubt that physical health is enhanced by the
mending of the spiritual life.

Nevertheless, the Psalmist says that God has crushed the very
life out of him. Perhaps it is easier to accept that God punishes
the wicked rather than harms the righteous, but then few of us
think of ourselves as wicked. Yet, the opposite may be the case
when we do encounter suffering. We may accept that, in some
mystery of providence, God may use suffering for the good of
all, just as we require people in the emergency services to face

death in order to rescue others. Suffering and misfortune may, in God's hands, bring sinners to their senses but can we really imagine that God wilfully crushes sinners with pain? Surprisingly, like the Psalmist, people often react to tragedy in this way for at least it seems to give our pain a purpose. Children feel they have done something wrong when their parents break up and patients with terminal illness will ask what they have done wrong as a possible explanation for indiscriminate suffering. So, the Psalmist voices this feeling that God has torn and broken our lives. This is how we see God, because both sin and sickness distort our image of God and project human feelings of anger and punishment. None of this is a reasoned doctrine of God. It is what we feel at the time, and the strength of the psalms is that they are not afraid to voice it in public.

In the prophets there is another message that must be taken alongside our anger: in all our suffering, whatever the cause, we are still held in the heart of God and our hurt causes God pain. The Lord tells us, 'For the hurt of my people I am hurt'; in their distress God is distressed and God's heart recoils with compassion from the just deserts of their sin (*cf.* Jer. 8.21; Isa. 63.9; Hos. 11.8). Where there is reproof, it comes only from the love that makes us specially dear to God (Prov. 3.12). God does not stand aloof from sin or pain for, if there is to be forgiveness, as Charles Williams understood, 'the two persons must coinhere in that mutual act, and pardon must be doubly welcome. Like joy (of which, at its best, it is a manifestation), it does not demand forgetfulness but acute knowledge.'[13]

The clothing of the spirit

Now the psalm begins to look forward to a new life with God, praying for a clean heart and a new and right spirit. Few verses have so influenced the worship of the Church. Once again, the Liturgy of Ash Wednesday sets before us in word and deed God's renewing grace. The Collect in the Anglican rite is based on a prayer from the Sarum service at the imposition of ashes:

Create and make in us new and contrite hearts
that we, worthily lamenting our sins
and acknowledging our wretchedness,
may receive from you, the God of all mercy,
perfect remission and forgiveness . . .

The ashes symbolize our frailty but also our hope, because they recall the dust from which God created us with the breath of life. Echoing the language of procreation ('within me' might be translated 'within my womb'), we pray for new life to be conceived in us.

Make me a clean heart, O God,
and renew a right spirit within me.
Cast me not away from your presence
and take not your holy spirit from me.
                              Psalm 51.10–12 (Common Worship)

There is a vulnerability in the Psalmist's prayer. Unburdening sin creates a vacuum and uncertainty about the future: we know that we cannot return to the old routine again. Even with sin confronted and healed, we are still aware of a nakedness like Adam and Eve in the garden. The past security of pride and arrogance is gone: the way ahead is fraught with dangers we previously ignored. The cleansed heart is not an end in itself but a preparation for the indwelling of God who empowers us to live a life of grace, sometimes expressed in the metaphor of clothing. In the Jewish *Targum of Genesis* (3.21) we find God clothed Adam and Eve not in garments of skin ('*or*) but a clothing of glory or, as one Hebrew manuscript of the Bible is said to have read, garments of light ('*or*).

From such sources the Syrian Church developed a rich symbolism of the robe of glory which God gives us to redeem our fallible nakedness and restore in us the divine image marred by Adam and Eve.[14]

It was Christ who was able to reclothe them
in the glory they had stripped off, thus replacing the
    leaves.
                                      Ephrem: Nat. 1.43

Like Cyril of Jerusalem, Ephrem the Syrian interprets Jesus' curse on the fig tree as a sign that his saving work will render the covering of our shame with its leaves redundant. The idea of spiritual clothing naturally appears in the preparation of the priest for the Eucharist in many traditions and the words of Psalms 51 and 93 have inspired accompanying prayers. In the Armenian liturgy, the vesting prayer is addressed to the Holy Spirit, whose whole work of empowering in creation is recalled as the priest prepares to celebrate the new creation of the Eucharist:

> O mystery, deep, unsearchable, eternal,
> who has decked with splendid glory the heavenly
> powers . . .
> with wondrous power you created Adam in a lordly
> image,
> and clothed him with gracious glory in the garden of
> Eden . . .
> O chalice of fiery rain that was poured on the apostles
> in the holy upper room,
> O Holy Spirit, pour your wisdom on us also
> with the vestment:
> Holiness becomes your house, who are clothed with
> majesty.

Our recovery of paradise is fulfilled in the incarnation of Christ and these prayers and psalms, which remind us of the Spirit's overshadowing of Mary, speak to us not only of an outer clothing but an inner presence which is ours by our baptism.

> Whereas the river in which Christ was baptized
> was clothed in light from within;
> so too did Mary's body, in which He resided,
> gleam from within.

> See, Fire and Spirit in the womb that bore You,
> see, Fire and Spirit in the river in which You were
> baptized.

Fire and Spirit in our Baptism,
in the Bread and the Cup, Fire and the Holy Spirit.
Ephrem: Church 36.6; Faith 10.17

Our communion with Christ is a mutual bond whereby our body is Christ's clothing and his Spirit is our robe (Ephrem: Nat. 22.39). This awesome image of not only being clothed with God but God being clothed with us draws us to the remarkable perceptiveness of Hebrew Scripture. Job can defend the integrity of his faith because 'I put on righteousness and she clothed herself in me' (Job 29.14). It is the Spirit of the Lord who 'clothes herself' with prophets like Gideon, Amasai and Zechariah to challenge idolatry and restore the true God into people's lives (Judg. 6.34; 1 Chron. 12.18; 2 Chron. 24.20).

The Psalmist brings together these perspectives of the Spirit. The Spirit is the outer garment, the joy of salvation (*cf.* Isa. 66), our renewed image in the presence (literally, face) of God, but also the creative, indwelling power of God within us, sustaining us with life. Meditating on this mystery before communion has seemed so important that the prayers of the priest vesting have partly passed into devotions for the laity, reflecting the need for all the people of God to be prepared. We can already see this in the way the eighth-century Greek hymn 'O Heavenly King, Comforter' (*Basileu Ouranie*) appears both in the rite of preparation before the liturgy and yet has become part of people's individual prayers. As a prayer to 'the Spirit of Truth' to cleanse us and save our souls, it seems to echo Psalm 51. In the Anglican communion the Collect for Purity has become a similar prayer of preparation. Attributed to Gregory, abbot of Canterbury (also in the eighth century), it appears in the Sarum rite which began with asperging the congregation while the psalm was sung. The celebrant and assistants retired to vest for Mass and the Office of Terce was sung by the choir, including the Office Hymn 'Come, Holy Ghost, our souls inspire' (*Veni Creator Spiritus*) which became part of the priest's own preparation. There followed a versicle and the prayer which has become so familiar:

V   Send forth your Spirit and they will be created.
R   *And you will renew the face of the earth.*

Almighty God, to whom all hearts are open, all desires
known, and from whom no secrets are hidden: cleanse the
thoughts of our hearts by the inspiration of your Holy Spirit,
that we may perfectly love you and worthily magnify your
holy name . . .

The prayer takes up the Hebrew meaning of Spirit as 'breath',
the most intimate and vital relationship of internal organs and
external environment. A similar Syrian meditation draws on the
Psalmist's desire for God to create a pure heart 'so that, through
the power of your Spirit, I may inhale your salvation'.[15] The
Sarum collect is now adopted in Anglican rites worldwide as a
preparation for the whole congregation at the Eucharist and, just
as the priest's vesting is a reminder of ordination, so this devotion
may recall that we are all clothed with Christ in baptism by the
Holy Spirit (Gal. 3.17). A wider use of Psalm 51 privately said
before worship would nurture a refreshing awareness of God's
creative presence changing and moulding us.

Restoring the picture

As God's presence fills our being, the Spirit begins the work of
restoration.

> Restore to me the joy of your salvation,
>   and sustain me with your kindly spirit.
>
> *Psalm 51.12*

In Hebrew the prayer for God to restore us (*hashivah*) mirrors
our turning to God in repentance (*t'shuvah*). We are cleansed and
renewed but not changed into something totally alien to our
nature, for the Holy Spirit recovers for us the image of God with
which we were created. A helpful parallel is the rediscovery of
the spiritual through ikons which throw light on the meaning
of all sacred art.

> For such a work to be original . . . it has to express or
> reveal such an origin; and what is meant when it is said that
> a work of sacred art possesses originality is not that there is

something new about it but that it is a faithful image of an archetype.[16]

In baptism we find a direct comparison with art using the image of restoring a picture, for here, as in painting, oil and water cooperate to effect the transformation. The most remarkable example of this theology is in fact a work of art. On the epitaph from the third-century tomb of Callixtus in Rome we see the image of a dove apparently holding a paintbrush with its foot and inscribing the Chi-Rho monogram, indicating that the departed was baptized into Christ by the Holy Spirit. Ephrem develops the idea more vividly in a hymn depicting the restorer using oil to clean away the dirt inherited from generations, and revealing the image of God underneath.

> A royal portrait is painted with visible colours,
> and with oil that all can see
> is the hidden portrait of our hidden King
> portrayed on those who have been signed;
> on them Baptism, that is in travail with them in its womb,
> depicts the new portrait,
> to replace the image of the former Adam which was
>   corrupted.[17]

The Spirit seeks to recover our originality rather than replace it and, similarly, evangelism has no business suppressing our true selves but should awaken our humanity in all its wonder.

> You cleanse everything
> From the stain on its earthly beauty,
> Wiping away sins
> And anointing wounds.
> In all these ways your life shines forth,
> Wakening and re-awakening everything to life.[18]

Restoration does not take us back to a state before human sin, any more than a picture can be restored without any sign of its age. The marks of our sin and hurt are transfigured like the wounds on the risen body of Christ into a spiritually deeper inheritance that would not otherwise have been ours. The medieval Church in the West expressed this in the great Exsultet of the Easter Vigil, whose joy in the 'happy fault' of Adam remains alive and kicking in the Roman rite.

> O happy fault, O necessary sin of Adam,
> which gained for us so great a Redeemer!
> Most blessed of all nights, chosen by God
> to see Christ rising from the dead!

Our sins and their forgiveness are part of our spiritual growth and, by God's grace, they may even bring joy to others. In the ultimate economy of God, Julian of Norwich sees that 'sin shall be no shame but worship to human beings': there is 'for every sin . . . a bliss by love'.[19]

Repairing the world

With the renewal of our lives comes the restoration of our calling. Once again we know that we are valued in God's service. The Psalmist's plea not to be sent away is the prayer of one who has often been sent on the Lord's business. Forgiveness is the moment when God also commissions us to be messengers of good news. This is implicit in the introspective atmosphere of Ash Wednesday as we sing:

> Then I shall teach your ways to the wicked
> and sinners shall return to you.
> Deliver me from my guilt, O God,
>   the God of my salvation,
> and my tongue shall sing of your righteousness.
> O Lord, open my lips,
> and my mouth shall proclaim your praise.
>   *Psalm 51.13–15* (Common Worship)

We are not preaching to others from any moral superiority, nor are we judging them or patronizing them. We are simply one with Christ who joined sinners in their quest for renewal at his baptism and consistently showed solidarity with them. The Jewish Hasidic tradition is just as strong in believing that we should support those who fail.

God does not look on the evil part of our life . . . how
should I dare to? Whoever passes judgment on a person has
passed it on themselves . . . Whoever separates themselves
from the sinner departs from that situation with guilt. But
the saint can suffer for the sin of another person as their
own . . . Only living with the other is justice . . . Living
with the other as a form of knowing is justice. Living with
the other as a form of being is love.[20]

This calling is illustrated in the parting words of the Christian
priest to a penitent at confession, 'Pray also for me, a sinner',
reversing their roles. Here the penitent is immediately called
back to their part in rebuilding a broken world and praying for
those who err, including the priest who has just given them
absolution. This solidarity of brokenness may explain why Psalm
51 continues to stress that sorrow for our sin and humility before
God are more acceptable and perhaps more fruitful than ritual
sacrifice.

For you desire no sacrifice, else would I give it;
you take no delight in burnt-offerings.
The sacrifice of God is a broken spirit;
a broken and contrite heart, O God, you will not despise.
Psalm 51.16–17 (Common Worship)

Brueggemann rightly complains that the interpretation of
these words had often been narrow and reductionist: 'the
brokenness may not be a psychological dismantling . . . it may
well be an economic unburdening, a political risking, a stepping
away from whatever form of power we have used by which to
secure ourselves'.[21]

The psalm's last verses, dismissed by some as a later addition,
prove the point. David concluded a confession from a broken
heart with a prayer for the rebuilding of his community. The 'I'
of the Psalmist speaks for a whole society: if one suffers, all
suffer. Today we individualize sin so that, while retaining our
precious privacy, we offer no solidarity to those who fall but only
make them the more wary of opening up to a self-righteous
world. Yet there are parts of the liturgy such as the peace or the

breaking of bread where 'sign-acts' of corporate reconciliation could be explored.[22]

Priest   The sacrifice of God must be a broken spirit.
R   *Our broken and contrite heart, O God, you will not*
          despise.
          First make good our lives for your pleasure in this
          holy place:
R   *Repair the walls of our community.*
          Then you will find joy in our sacrifice,
R   *A whole offering of our life, lived in justice.*
                        cf. *Psalm 51.17–19 (Responsory at the Peace)*

We let God place us in the ruined landscape of hurt and despair between sinner and sinned against. 'I cry you mercy, Lord . . . for all the people in this world', prayed Margery Kempe, 'that you make their sins to me, by true contrition, as it were my own sins, and forgive them as I would that you forgave me.'[23]

With his theory of co-inherence, Charles Williams takes this bonding beyond reconciliation. Moved by the story of Felicitas in prison, who told her jailer that she would be able to suffer greater pain in her martyrdom because 'then another will be in me who will suffer for me, as I shall suffer for him', he describes a way of life that can rebuild society. People take upon themselves responsibility for others and sometimes take up the burdens and guilt of others, following the kind of substitutionary love which we feed on in the Eucharist and which Christ lives through us. Our own acts of forgiving are part of this. 'The injured bears the trouble of another's sin; he who is forgiven receives the freedom of another's love.'[24] And in forgiveness there is more mutual give and take than we acknowledge. Otherwise it is overbearing and patronizing. In a more secular setting, Williams finds this message again and again in the plays of Shakespeare where characters can only further their own desires by intervening on behalf of others.

So, the final verses of Psalm 51 with their call to tell of God's grace and rebuild society make us realize, as Henri Nouwen said, 'that there is a call beyond the call to return. It is the call to

become the Father who welcomes home and calls for a celebration. Having reclaimed my sonship, I now have to claim
fatherhood . . . I now see that the hands that forgive, console,
heal, and offer a festive meal must become my own.'[25] We are
back to where the Psalmist began, with the faithful love of the
Divine Mother, Father, whose compassion is now the love with
which we parent others.

SIX

The Dew of the Dawn

Son of the dawn

The born-again teenager who wants to declare their faith in Jesus as their personal Saviour and be baptized by total immersion and the mother who rings up the vicar almost casually to book a date for the christening have more in common than either of them would probably want to admit. Both seek some public witness in a holy place and both want to claim God's special love for them in a way that affirms their body and whole person at a time when these are changing. In the parent's case, they are claiming this for their child, the fruit of their body. Now that the baby is physically separate from the mother, they feel a need for the child's own identity to be recognized in the community and for God's love for the child to be declared. The teenager, developing their identity as they move away from the parental realm, has a not dissimilar need to be accepted for themselves.

In Israel, that unique acceptance of the individual by God was represented by their anointed king, so often celebrated in the psalms, which traditionally were called the Psalms of David. The music of the Temple worship is said to have been commissioned and organized by the king and even the 4000 instruments are attributed to his design! (1 Chr. 15; 23.4–5). His successor, Solomon, is also noted as a composer of hymns (1 Kings 5.12; cf. Pss. 72, 127). The royal tradition continued with Hezekiah who re-organized the music and ritual of the worship (2 Chr. 29.25–30; cf. Isa. 38.9–20). Some scholars have rejected this evidence and dated the psalms mostly to a post-exilic period but

the thorough work of Birkeland and Eaton has shown that so far
from the so-called individual psalms being the prayer of some
anonymous worshipper, they presuppose an intimate relationship
with God characteristic of the king.[1]

With the changing of seasons and political fortunes the
religious and social status of the sovereign had to be re-affirmed.
From the practice of surrounding nations Israel took up the ritual
of the king being acclaimed as divinely born or adopted at an
autumn enthronement festival. Psalm 2 seems to set out the
stages of this rite, as the king was first anointed, enthroned, then
presented with a decree containing the title deeds of his divine
sonship and world sovereignty, and finally he received a kiss of
submission from his vassals.

The first Christian preachers found in this psalm not only the
victory of the resurrection but the belief that the Messiah,
the Son of God, reflected from the beginning the glory of God,
for he shared the character of God's own being (Luke 20.41–4;
Acts 13.33; Heb. 1.1–5; 5.5–6). Thus it came into the Christmas
liturgy as the Introit at Midnight Mass in the Roman rite and, in
the Byzantine liturgy, as the verses which herald the Epistle (Heb.
1.1–12), itself inspired by the Psalmist's hymn.

> The Lord said to me: You are my Son,
> I have begotten you today.
> Ask of me and I will give you the nations
> for your inheritance.

Psalm 110 also seems to have been composed for the king's
enthronement: divine sonship and universal rule are proclaimed
by an oracle which identifies the sovereignty of the Lord with the
sovereignty of the king on earth. Here the king's sacred character
is shown by him appearing freshly anointed with oil, described in
Ugaritic and Hebrew writing as 'the dew of heaven' (Gen.
27.28). The image of a king as a 'son of the dawn' (Isa. 14.12)
and the use of oil as a symbol of rebirth from the dust of death
(Isa. 26.19) indicate the eternal privilege of the anointed, a
theme which would have been even more powerfully illustrated
if the anointing took place at the Gihon spring with its associations of paradise.

The word of the Lord for my lord.
'Sit at my right hand
until I make your enemies
a footstool for your feet . . .
With you is noble grace
on this day of your birth,
in holy splendour from the womb of the dawn;
upon you is the dew of your fresh life.'

The king is acclaimed and appropriately vested as a royal priest like the ancient king of Jerusalem.

'You are a priest for ever
after the order of Melchizedek.'

Psalm 110.4 (cf. *Gen.14.19*)

His intimacy with God as a son in his father's house meant that he naturally organized the Temple liturgy, leading new songs of praise with his own accompaniment of stringed instruments (Pss. 92.1–4; 144.9–10). He wore the priestly *ephod* and led the dancing procession that brought the Ark into the Temple where he prayed for blessing (Pss. 45.2; 118.26–7; 132 *cf.* 2 Sam. 6.14–15). Ideally, he offered the sacrifices in person while the people prayed for God to accept them (Ps. 20 *cf.* 1 Kings 3.4). As the special servant of the Lord, he elevated the cup at communion feasts (Ps. 116). After the Exile, his liturgical role was assumed by the high priest who wore his vesture, was anointed like the king and even shared the royal throne and crown (*cf.* Exod. 28.36–8; Lev. 8.12; 21.12; Ps. 133.2; Zech 6.9–13).

The Letter to the Hebrews expounds Jesus' own ministry in these terms and the quotations from Psalms 2 and 110 affirm that this priest is also recognized as Son of God. The Byzantine Christmas liturgy spells out this eternal relationship with God and the eternal effectiveness of Christ's priesthood:

From the womb before the Morning Star
I have begotten you.
The Lord has sworn and will not change it:
You are a priest for ever after the order of Melchizedek.

Son of God, born of a virgin,
save us who sing to you, alleluia!

Contemplation of the calling

Such a typological approach to these texts has been widely
challenged and we have to admit that Christians have often
forced dogmatic interpretations on Hebrew Scripture with a
total disregard for Jewish scholarship. But the more we look at
the Jewish background of psalmody, the more we may discover
how it shaped Jesus' prayer and sense of calling and can form
ours also.

The paradox of this unfolding relationship for Jesus is that, as
with parent and child, the Son is allowed to discover his identity
within the mystery of God and yet remain other than the Father.
Nothing could express more fully the generosity of God's grace,
as the Indian contemplative Abhishiktananda explains:

> To use the metaphor of Psalm 110, it is like the divine and
> eternal 'dawn' of the Son's coming forth from the bosom of
> Yahweh; for the Son is wholly from the Father alone, and is
> absolutely nothing except what the Father is; yet he is *other
> than* the Father, and his entire 'right to be' is implicit in the
> very being of the Father.
>
> In the depth of this total void, of which only Being and
> nothingness are capable, and indeed in the 'silence' of
> being, there can be heard the *Thou* which eternally calls the
> Son into being. In the utterance of that Word which fills
> eternity, Being awakes to itself in its own Source, which is
> the Father . . . All his awareness of himself is constituted
> by the *Thou* which he hears the Father pronounce: 'Thou
> art my beloved son; today "this day" of eternity and of a
> timeless present, I have begotten thee.'[2]

The kings of Israel often reflected on their own vocation,
spending the night in prayer in the Temple as they wrestled with
the prosperity of the wicked and the suffering of the righteous.

Answer me when I call, O God of my righteousness . . .

> How long will you nobles dishonour my glory? . . .
> There are many that say, 'Who will show us any
>   good?' . . .
> Lord, lift up the light of your countenance upon us.
>
> *Psalm 4, Compline* (Common Worship)

We see Solomon at night at Gibeon, a place of sacrifice, receiving a dream of promise from God and in the Psalter the king finds instruction as he keeps vigil with the Lord always before him: before God he can examine his own soul and see his enemies in perspective like ghosts in a dream (1 Kings 3.5; Pss. 4, 16, 17, 73). His vigil is filled with the light of God's revelation, transforming his inner darkness and reminding him of his special calling since the dawn of time when humankind was created out of mother earth.

> Yea, the darkness is no darkness with thee,
>   but the night is as clear as the day . . .
> thou hast covered me in my mother's womb.
> I will give thanks unto thee,
>   for I am fearfully and wonderfully made:
> marvellous are thy works, and that my soul knoweth right
>   well.
> My bones are not hid from thee:
> though I be made secretly, and fashioned beneath in the
>   earth . . .
> When I wake up I am present with thee.
>
> *Psalm 139.12–15, 17* (BCP)

For Jesus, too, times of contemplation and sleep are occasions of divine revelation and his disciples also experienced this at the threshold of waking and sleeping (Luke 9.18; Mark 4.38–41; Luke 9.32). Already as he prepares to enter adult life, he delights in exploring the Scriptures with the teachers in the Temple and it is here that he seems to become aware of his special relationship with God (Luke 2.49). According to the same Lucan tradition, it is at times of prayer that Jesus' vocation and identity are disclosed both to himself and others and, at the Baptism and Transfiguration, the words of Psalm 2 are formative in the mind of Jesus (Luke 3.21–2; 9.18–20, 28–35).

When confrontation becomes imminent, the psalms encourage Jesus as he faces the inevitability of God's chosen servant being killed (Mark 12.1–12 cf. Pss. 80, 118). Teaching in the Temple itself, Jesus turns to Psalm 110 in an enigmatic discussion, further obfuscated by the evangelist. Yet it is clear from the whole context of Mark 12 that Jesus is challenging political and religious authority which preempts the sovereignty of God. Scholars have concluded that the real question of the debate is not who the Messiah is but what his role should be.[3] Jesus avoids the term 'Son of David' which could mislead Jewish expectations and confuse Gentiles, preferring 'Son of Man' with its implication that divine sonship involves being part of a human community and taking responsibility for their sin (cf. 2 Sam. 7. 12–17).

Children of God

However intimate this relationship may be, the analogy of son and father has become difficult in a society of broken families. Equally problematic is the patriarchal model of God which has distorted our understanding of God and the world. In sermons and Bible studies the cultural context of Scripture can be explained but with the psalms the issue is more difficult, because, as liturgical texts, they go unchallenged as we sing them and subconsciously form our life of prayer.

Yet anthropomorphic symbols seem to be important for us, reflecting a need for personal encounter and commitment. 'To erase gender from our image of God . . . can tend towards a neutrality of prayer.'[4] Apparently inclusive language may divorce us from the reality of relationships; we never address anyone as 'parent' to their face. We cannot redeem false conceptions of gender if we abandon it altogether. As we read the stories of the biblical patriarchs, we may also conclude that the father–son relationship has always been a problem. 'To give up God as "Father" is not only to give up male privilege . . . it also seems to mean giving up on the search for our own fathers, and that is difficult to do, for we know how deeply we long to reconnect with them.'[5] Any hope of reconciling the world with itself rests with restoring an ikon of God as the archetype of human relationships. In psalmody, alongside the father image we find God as the mother, the womb and well of life who brings forth creation (Pss. 36.7–9; 90.1–2), sustaining us with compassion from the womb and weaning us like children growing to maturity (Pss. 25.6; 51.1; 86.15; 145.9; 131). She is the Wisdom of the Law, the Torah, our companion and counsellor, the breath of the Spirit who brings creation to life (Ps. 19 *cf.* Prov. 8; Pss. 119.24, 54, 97; 104.30). She is the midwife who brings us out from the pain of labour to new hope (Pss. 22.9–11; 71.6).

> The very range of possible imagery forbids us to *identify* God with any limited form of words. We have a model for this practice in the Hebrew psalms, and in the long but often submerged tradition of Christian mysticism. In both, we find not only a wealth of exuberant but provisional imagery, but also a distinctive blend of the passionate and the political, that can express the integration of our desire.[6]

The role of kingship in psalmody is more difficult and it has been argued that it reflects an ideology of divine right which could function as a 'cover-up for a regime that forsook the memory of hurt and the vocation of compassion'.[7] Kings could use the liturgy to consecrate the *status quo* of despotism. The Zairean Mass, a showpiece of inculturation with its celebrant chief in goatskin hat and spear-bearing acolytes, is an example of male power-symbolism ousting other African values such as the spirituality of the assembly or the symbolism of offering.[8] We should not, however, just identify the royal psalms as those with a hierarchical style. The relationship of God and the king involved experiences of intimacy akin to a parent sitting up all night with a teenager rather than a tyrant. The royal psalms of triumph cannot be separated from the laments of a leader pleading for his people in danger.

The importance of such imagery is that, at its best, it forms a model which challenges secular authority with the authority of God. In his work on texts such as Psalms 45 and 72, Raymond

Tournay has brought a welcome eschatological dimension. On
the face of it, we have there a eulogy of the monarch and his
princess, an ikon of Solomon in all his wisdom and beauty, but is
it 'a question of the historical Solomon or of the new Solomon,
the ruler-messiah?'[9] Could not the worshippers see beyond the
propaganda to pray for an anointed servant of God who would
one day defend the weak and give the poor justice? Were the
people of Israel not sufficiently mature to believe that God could
raise up such a leader, even if their hopes were sometimes dashed
by kings who failed them? Reject this liturgical tradition out of
hand and we may divorce our image of God from the reality
of political struggle, which is as dangerous as identifying the two.

The sanctity of anointing was not only bestowed on kings.
The patriarchs are protected by God as 'my anointed ones,
my prophets' (Ps. 105,15). The oil flowing down Aaron's face
symbolizes the grace and solidarity of the priesthood (Ps. 133).
Anointed by the Lord, the prophet Isaiah tells the people that
they are to be called priests of the Lord, fulfilling their divine
calling at Sinai to be 'a kingdom of priests and a holy nation' (Isa.
61; Exod. 19.6) and the ritual reserved for the king becomes a
metaphor of vocation for the whole community:

> You came forth to save your people,
> to save your anointed.
>
> *Habakkuk 3.13*

Jesus follows this path, first identifying his calling with those
gathered for baptism by the Jordan. He sees himself as Isaiah's
prophet anointed by the Spirit to bring good news to the poor
yet shares his ministry with disciples who are called and set
apart for mission. Through the prayer he teaches them, they are
initiated into the intimate father–son relationship of the Anointed
One of God, the prerogative of Israel's king (Ps. 89.26). Their
spiritual enlightenment is described as rebirth, begotten of God
like the Hebrew king (John 3.3; 1.12–13).

For the Early Church baptism was the symbol of that unique
relationship with God. Drawing on the image of the vine in the
gospel and the olive-tree in Paul, Cyril of Jerusalem tells us that
by our baptismal anointing we have become 'partakers of the

richness of the true olive-tree' and 'likewise are called christs, of whom God said, "Do not touch my christs (anointed ones)" ' (Ps. 105.15).[10]

Despite Paul's theology of the baptized who could pray in the Spirit 'Abba, Father', Christendom often lost sight of our filial relationship with God. Yet the third-century Syrian Church could celebrate baptism with the bishop proclaiming over the newly initiated the royal oracle, 'You are my son: this day I have begotten you.' (Ps. 2.7)[11] A century later, we find this intimacy with God developed in the spirituality of '*ihidaya*', an untranslateable term that has the sense of the uniqueness, single-mindedness and integration of a person. Just as it used of the only-begotten Son of the Father (John 1.14; 3.16), so it comes to describe the individual disciple who shares the uniqueness of God's Anointed. The Persian theologian Aprahat speaks of 'the Ihidaya [Christ] from the bosom of the Father giving joy to all the *ihidaya* [the followers of Christ]'.[12] The baptismal rite of the Church of England has restored this theme of our adoption as God's sons and daughters in its accompanying psalmody:

> 'I have found David my servant;
> with my holy oil have I anointed him.
> My hand shall hold him fast
> and my arm shall strengthen him . . .
> He shall call to me, "You are my Father,
> my God, and the rock of my salvation;"
> And I will make him my firstborn . . .'
> *Psalm 89.21–2, 27–8* (Common Worship)

A royal priesthood

Through anointing the Church also identified with the priesthood of Christ, for we continue to be Christ's presence in the world. Tertullian draws a direct parallel with the priests of Israel:

> Then, having come up from the font, we are thoroughly anointed with a blessed unction, in accordance with the ancient discipline, whereby, since the time when Aaron was anointed by Moses, people used to be anointed to the

priesthood with oil from a horn. From this you are called 'christs' after the chrism which also lent its name to the Lord.[13]

The language of royal priesthood in the baptismal sermon of 1 Peter already makes it clear that this is a corporate calling of the whole body of Christ.

In the Maundy Thursday rite for the Blessing of the Oils Psalm 133 has been used to depict our vocation. Its rich imagery has proved irresistable to many theologians, including Ambrose who finds in it a paradigm of how the community of the Church grows in faith.

> Understand why this anointing is done, because the eyes of the wise person are in their head. It then flowed down the beard, that is, to the grace of youth, even to Aaron's beard, that you may become a chosen race, priestly and precious. For we are all anointed with spiritual grace to the kingdom of God and a shared priesthood (*consacerdotium*).[14]

The psalm was also sung in the medieval Sarum rite as a newly consecrated bishop was received by the diocese or a new dean was installed in the cathedral, kneeling before the cross and surrounded by the chapter.[15]

Ordination is the sacrament where we would expect anointed priesthood and shared vocation to be inextricably bound together, for ordained priests have no vocation apart from the Church. The psalmody in the Roman rite, however, stresses the singularity of offering the eucharistic sacrifice. Anglican and Episcopal rites of North America reflect the more inter-dependent theology of Psalm 132, originally found in the Armenian Ordination service. The king brings the Ark of the Covenant home and the whole congregation join in its blessing: here is a community where resources are shared with all.

> I will surely bless her provisions,
>   and satisfy her poor with bread.
> I will clothe her priests with salvation,
>   and her faithful people will rejoice and sing.

There will I make the horn of David flourish;
I have prepared a lamp for my anointed . . .
Let your priests be clothed with righteousness,
Let your faithful people sing with joy.
                    Psalm 132.15–17 (Canadian Anglican Ordination)

The privilege of our relationship with God gives us a special
responsibility for the marginalized. Though the royal psalms may
attract criticism for their blessing on secular power, they have a
vision of the world which transcended their historical setting and
carries an authentic message from age to age. In his campaign
against slavery, child labour and gambling, the editor of a Sheffield newspaper paraphrased Psalm 72 to proclaim the society of
justice which God's Anointed comes to create.

Hail to the Lord's Anointed,
    Great David's greater Son!
Hail, in the time appointed,
    His reign on earth begun!
He comes to break oppression,
    To set the captive free,
To take away transgression
    And rule in equity.

                                   James Montgomery (1821)

The brutalized Christians of El Salvador saw in this psalm a
challenge to authority, rather than its legitimization, rejoicing
that the faithful have woken up to their calling to defend the weak
instead of just saying masses for the executed.

He shall rule from sea to sea,
from the Great River to earth's bounds,
his foes shall lick the dust.

                                        Psalm 72.8–9

My Church has chosen, she has decided.
She has decided in favour of her neighbour.
She has chosen the other person.
She has decided for the one who is far off.
She has entered the world of conflicts . . .
                            Litany in time of need (1980)

The liturgical role of this psalm in Masses for Peace and Justice was not lost on the Church there. For all of us 'the royal psalms remind us forcefully that to have power means to empower others to a genuinely human life'.[16] Jesus pointed out that for David himself the royal prerogative involved giving priority to feeding the hungry over the laws of the sanctuary (Mark 2.25–6).

Living our calling

The struggle to live the life of the kingdom appears in the symbolism surrounding baptismal anointing, where the newly baptized are depicted as wrestlers against evil. The Syrian hymn writer Ephrem finds an inventive parallel in the world of pearl-divers who oil their bodies before plunging down into the depths to find the pearl of great price. Elsewhere, he compares the anointing of the baptized with Christ's baptism of death and resurrection both in its cost of discipleship and in the immortality of what seemed mortal humanity:

> Oil in its love accompanies the baptized in his need,
> when, despising his life,
> he descends and buries himself in the water:
> oil by its nature cannot die,
> yet He clothed himself in a mortal body,
> he was baptized, and so raised up from the water
> a treasure of life for the race of Adam.
>
> H Virg 7.10[17]

The undying quality of oil implies an enduring, immortal quality about a human body consecrated to God. The Hebrew taboo marking out the king's body was one that even David would not break when his own life was threatened. Likewise, our bodies anointed in baptism are the temple of the Holy Spirit. Nowhere is this physical sanctity more explicit than in marriage whose vocation Eastern Christendom has affirmed since at least the fourth century by crowning the bride and groom. The ceremony later drew on the poetry of the Psalmist who sees that in the anointed king all humanity shares in the privilege of a special relationship with God.

> Lord our God, crown them with glory and honour.
> You have set upon their heads crowns of precious stones.
> Life they sought from you and you gave it to them.
>
> cf. *Psalms 8.5; 21.4*

The royalty we have is not about domination but a reflection of the divine nature. 'The king which rules us from within is that which is called the image of God and upon this God has placed his glory and splendour' notes a Syrian commentator on the psalms.[18] The couple are crowned and drink from a common cup, expressing the communion and creativity of divine love in which we share.

> O God, you created all things by your strength. You established the world and adorned the crown of all that you had made. Bless also with a spiritual blessing this common cup which you give to those united in the communion of marriage.

The victorious martyrs (literally 'witnesses') join with Mary in the universal rejoicing of the couple who themselves will witness to the love which conquers all. Eastern rites delight in the joy of marriage with sensuous language also taken from the royal psalms. The Coptic wedding draws to a close with the chorus 'The king desires your beauty' (Ps. 45.11), a refrain also found in the Armenian rite at the beginning of a service to remove the crowns of the couple. In Egypt, a similar ceremony is equally unrestrained:

> The king shall rejoice in your strength, O Lord:
>   how greatly he exults in your salvation.
> You have given him his heart's desire
>   and you have not denied him the request of his lips.
>
> *Psalm 21.1–2 (Tajlisa Ceremony)*

The royal symbolism of these rites opens up a wider perspective where the physical joy of marriage is seen in the realm of God's whole creative purpose. This is in contrast to many Western weddings which have tended to become a time of incestuous self-congratulation.

The vocation of the Christian in the world is just as important in the area of sickness, which has largely been privatized into a relationship dependant on professionals, whether counsellors, priests, doctors or nurses. We rightly seek the grace of the Holy Spirit in the sacraments when we are ill, but how often do patients see themselves as called to bear witness? Alexander Schmemann, the Orthodox theologian, has taken issue with this attitude and given us an insight into what anointing of the sick may mean.

> Here is a man suffering on his bed of pain and the Church comes to him to perform the sacrament of healing. For this man, as for everyone and the whole world, suffering can be *the* defeat, the way of a complete surrender to darkness, despair and solitude. It can be *dying* in the very real sense of the word. And yet it can be also the ultimate victory of Man and of Life in him. The Church does not come to restore *health* in this man, simply to replace medicine when medicine has exhausted its own possibilities. The Church comes to take this man into the Love, the Light and the Life of Christ. It comes not merely to 'comfort' him in his sufferings, not to 'help' him, but make him a *martyr*, witness to Christ in his very sufferings.[19]

This is not news to patients with AIDS or terminal cancer who often receive great strength from the solidarity, courage and hope of others who are some way ahead of them on the journey and who embody the victory of the human person over death.

In the Greek Orthodox Church this call to live Christ for others is declared every year on the Wednesday of Holy Week at the public celebration of the Liturgy of the Holy Oil. Among the seven gospel readings in the service we hear of Zacchaeus, for whom salvation means openness to public mockery and restitution to the poor, and of the healing of Peter's mother-in-law followed by a warning to be ready to leave family ties. But there is also joy in the experience of God's mercy (underlined by the words 'mercy' and 'olive oil' having the same root in Greek), a joy which is to be sung and shared:

Alleluia! I will sing of mercy and justice to you, O Lord.

Psalm 101.1

The Roman rite of Anointing turns to the testimony of a humiliated Hebrew king who becomes a source of strength and wisdom to his people not despite his struggle but because of it. In its Christian context we can see that transfiguring power in the Eucharist whereby, even in our weakness, Christ can live in us for others.

I sought the Lord and was heard . . .
Come, children, and hear me
that I may teach you the fear of the Lord . . .
The Lord is close to the broken-hearted;
those whose spirit is crushed God will save.
Taste and see that the Lord is good.

Psalm 34.4, 11, 18

The witness given by those who have found God in their need is depicted by the thirteenth-century Italian master Duccio when he painted Jesus anointing the eyes of the man born blind. Beside the painting of the healing he placed a picture of the Transfiguration where the blind man, now with sight restored, appears with the other disciples gazing up in gratitude and wonder at the light radiating from Christ.

One service for the dying draws on Psalm 31, the Jewish prayer before sleep, at the time of the anointing. The anxiety of the dying (and those who watch with them) is given a voice. The journey to a horizon beyond death is waymarked. The protecting strength of God's grace shines in the oil covering the frail body of the believer, its fragrance filling the room, a foretaste of paradise.

Incline your ear to me:
make haste to deliver me.
R   *Shine on your servant with the light of your love.*
Be my strong rock, and house of defence:
be my guide and lead me for your name's sake.
R   *Shine on your servant with the light of your love.*
I will be glad and rejoice in your mercy:
for you have redeemed me, O Lord God of truth.

R   *Shine on your servant with the light of your love.*
                                    (A Prayer Book for Australia)

All those present join together to voice the prayer of the dying and so fulfil the priesthood which members of the Church offer vicariously for each other and for the world. Here we find again the joy of a shared faith which often characterized the parting of early Christians. Augustine, for example, tells how, at the death of Monica, Euodius took up the Psalter and began to sing and the whole house echoed with the response of the psalm:

> I will sing of mercy and justice to you, O Lord.
>   *Psalm 101.1*[20]

The oil of gladness

Oil is a wonderful symbol for this grace of God. Distinctive and undying, it distinguishes the special character of the person anointed. Upon a world smeared with toil, smudged with human sin and smell, the grandeur of God 'gathers to a greatness, like the ooze of oil crushed'.[21] Its flow is pervasive, overrunning human boundaries.

> See, how good and how lovely
> God's people who live together
> like brothers and sisters as one,
> like fragrant oil upon the head . . .
> flowing down onto the opening of the priest's robes,
> like the dew flowing down upon God's holy hill.
> For there the Lord has promised blessing, life to eternity.
>   *Psalm 133*

The free flowing of oil spells out the character of God's generous and unconditional love. Commenting on the parable of the wise and foolish bridesmaids, Gregory the Great describes the oil which the foolish go to buy as the 'oil of the sinner', a phrase from the Vespers Psalm, 141. Unlike the grace of God, this oil becomes merchandise that can be bought, accompanied by the obsequious persuasion of the seller and the bartering pride of the buyer.[22]

God alone is the source of this free grace and its unbounded, all-embracing nature is shown in the lavish extravagance and permeating fragrance of costly perfume, such as might be used at a coronation.

> Therefore God, your God, has anointed you
> with oil of gladness beyond your fellows.
> Myrrh and aloes with cassia are all your robes.
> From courts inlaid with ivory
> the music of strings fills you with joy.
>
> *Psalm 45.7–8*

The anointed king naturally led the song, for he was 'the lord of the dance and first minstrel of God'.[23] At the Roman Chrism Mass the bishop still recalls how 'the prophet David sang of the life and joy that the holy oil would bring us in the sacrament of your love'.

The heart of this joy is God's love which pours out in the desire to create and to care for creation. It is a love which is shown in God's trust, giving us stewardship of the world in all its wonder. And all of this calls for a day set apart in praise of our Maker. Psalm 92 is one of the ancient hymns for the Sabbath: the Midrash depicts Adam singing it after his first night on earth! Oil is a sign of spiritual strength and the joy of God's children in their Creator.

> For You have made me glad by Your deeds, O Lord;
> I sing for joy at Your handiwork . . .
> The brutish man cannot know it,
> The fool cannot understand it.
> Though the wicked flourish like grass, and all evildoers
> thrive,
> it is only that they may be destroyed for ever.
> But You, O Lord, are eternally on high.
> See, O Lord, Your enemies, see, how Your enemies
> perish;
> all evildoers are scattered.

But You exalted my strength like that of a wild ox;
I am anointed with ever-fresh oil.

(Inauguration of the Sabbath, ADPB)

With this proclamation of God's sovereignty 'it is as if we have burst through a circle of evil to emerge on the other side in the presence of God'.[24] Yet, despite the vision, the evildoers are very much part of the reality we have to deal with. Our privilege from God cannot be assumed: grace must flow and be worked into human society if goodness and dignity are to grow.

The righteous shall flourish like the palm tree,
and grow tall like the cedar in Lebanon,
Planted in the house of the Lord,
they shall blossom in the courts of our God.

(ADPB)

Just as the fresh oil filled the Temple with its perfume and the palm trees carved on the walls recalled God's creation completed for the first Sabbath, so this hymn looks from the beginning to the end of time, to the universal Sabbath of eternal life and peace which will have come through the defeat of evil and the growth of good.[25]

In today's Church where we seek the companionship of like-minded people, where baptism affirms the nuclear family at the cost of the universal people of God, where weddings just make use of a nice building, and the Eucharist has lost its symbolism as the Messianic feast for the poor, we have to rediscover the calling of being anointed as members of the Body of Christ. Our uniqueness will come to light when we share that gift with others. Only when the oil is released will a wounded world awake to its healing fragrance as we become the royal priesthood we are meant to be.

SEVEN

Descent into Darkness

Out of the depths

She had just lost her husband. I was greeted by the daughter who took me into the lounge and protested, 'I've told Mum she shouldn't keep on about Dad. It won't do her any good.' The television had been left on to fill any awkward silence with noise and distract the bereaved with its constantly changing images. I switched it off and gave her the space to talk about her husband. On the day of the funeral the daughter was the one person who could not face the service.

In the West we are not very good at grieving or allowing others to mourn, but the psalms give us permission. They express our human emotions with a disturbing realism, unless we are using a version from which some prissy editor has excised all the uncomfortable parts. When we feel ashamed of our feelings because they are 'unchristian', when we are unable to let go of our emotions for fear of upsetting others or losing control, the psalms come to our rescue and reassure us that we can pray the Word of God and still stay in touch with our real self.

One of the powerful images that comes out of bereavement or depression is that of the depths. The word expresses not only our sense of being hidden in some inaccessible place but the plural in Hebrew (*ma'amakim*) depicts wave upon wave of some uncontroll-able and destructive force which threatens to submerge our whole life in an element where we can hardly breathe. This helplessness needs to be voiced, especially at a funeral. In the Roman rite, our feeling of being overwhelmed surfaces in the liturgy at an earlier stage, as the family gathers around the body before it is taken into church. The body is sprinkled with holy water with all its ambiguity of meaning, drowning but renewing, and then the family pray:

> Out of the depths I cry to you, O Lord,
> Lord, hear my voice!
> O let your ears be attentive
> to the voice of my pleading.
>
> *Psalm 130 1–2*

The Psalmist knows well the feeling of 'going under' which sufferers from grief or depression recognize. There is a weariness and panic akin to the fear of a drowning person who feels that the forces against them are too strong. The experience of the deep is also taken up in Psalm 69 which the Church has traditionally used after the commemoration of the Last Supper on Maundy Thursday in a service known as Tenebrae (Darkness). In the service, at the end of each psalm a candle is extinguished. This loss of light seems to have been originally connected not with the coming of dawn but with Jesus' own inner darkness deepening with his sense of imminent betrayal in Gethsemane and the desertion of his friends.[1] As Jesus turned then to the psalms in his grief (Matt. 26.38 *cf*. Ps. 42.5, 11), we share our darkness with him, knowing, as he did, that someone has been there before.

Antiphon: I am wearied with all my crying as I await my God.
> Save me, O God:
> for the waters have risen to my neck.
> I have sunk into the mud of the deep:
> and there is no foothold.
> I have entered the waters of the deep:
> and the waves overwhelm me.
>
> *Psalm 69.1–2 (Maundy Thursday,*
> *Roman Office of Readings)*

Here, in the growing darkness and emptiness of the church on Maundy Thursday, stripped of its comforting symbols, we understand that our lives are pitted against some elemental force beyond personal misfortune. Death is the force that allows no escape but, at these times above all, we seek with Jesus a meaning for pain.

In his rejection he turned to the words of Psalm 22 to cry out in pain and rejection. Its descriptive phrases have inspired many artists to paint the psalm as an ikon of the Passion. Whether it is sung to symbolize the desertion of Gethsemane or the desolation of Golgotha, it helps us to know that Jesus shared the depths of physical and mental suffering and, through this psalm, we may share ours with him.

> But as for me, I am a worm and no man,
> scorned by all and despised by the people . . .
> I am poured out like water;
>   all my bones are out of joint;
> my heart has become like wax
>   melting in the depths of my body.
> My mouth is dried up like a pot-sherd;
>   my tongue cleaves to my gums;
> you have laid me in the dust of death.
> For the hounds are all about me,
>   the pack of evildoers close in on me;
> they pierce my hands and my feet.
> I can count all my bones;
>   they stand staring and looking upon me.
> *Psalm 22.6, 4–17 (Good Friday Gradual,* Common Worship)

The loss of human dignity is contrasted with the bestial imagery of the enemy, bulls, wild dogs and oxen, against which the victim is a worm. With any grief or depression, the body pays a heavy price. Sleeplessness and the effort of fighting mental pain leave us exhausted and paralyzed, scarcely able to put one foot in front of another: in such a state, asks the Psalmist, who can stand? Together with a breakdown of physical health, our self-image becomes poorer and poorer. The very resources we need to fight this battle desert us and we feel we have no foothold to grasp. And all around us, haunting sounds seem, by turns, to reflect and taunt our inner fear and insecurity. If this is our world, the Psalmist knows it well.

Dealing with anger

But the psalms take us further, plumbing the depths which we would prefer not to admit, let alone explore. Examining his own depression, Gonville ffrench-Beytagh concluded that:

> Perhaps the most acute mental sign is an utter loneliness and desolation which I am not able to describe. A lot of this is self-inflicted, because I have friends and could seek companionship, but somehow when I am in this state, I prefer to be alone and indulge in isolation and desolation. With this there goes an absolutely unreasoning, angry aggression, particularly to those close to me and whom I love. This ties up with what those psychiatrists say who maintain that all depression is repressed rage.[2]

If Christians find grief hard to express, we are lost when it comes to anger. All our upbringing teaches us to control and repress these negative and unchristian reactions. They are not acceptable in church or society. The pressures merely drive us further into the dark, as we mask our feelings and pretend to be what we are not. A young mother who lost her baby reacted for months and months with an amazingly defiant spirit, coping courageously for all the world to see. There seemed no way of ministering to her, indeed no need. Anger there was, but it was directed at the institution of the Church. It was a long time before she was ready to pour out her anger against God. While friends run around making cups of tea and trying to cheer us up, the psalms bring us to the point where we can shout out loud our cry of injustice, 'Why should it happen to me? What have I done to deserve this?' Like Job, they are not above telling God that our suffering is out of all proportion to any sin. Such protest carries hope for us: there is no faith worth the name unless it can face the worst.

One of the experiences which cries out with anger is the pain of the person who has been sexually abused as a child. It is in situations like this that the Christian tendency to plaster over the wounds rather than remove the pus is most damaging. Our unwillingness to face a justified sense of outrage adds years of repression. But when we are ready to acknowledge that anger, the psalms come to our aid as in this 'Liturgy for Women seeking Healing from Sexual Abuse'.

Leader   Can you turn now to God and speak of your anger and pain?

The following passages may be read by the person seeking healing, either alone or in unison with the other support people present.

> My God, my God, why have you abandoned me?
>> I have cried desperately for help,
>>> but still it docs not come.
> During the day I call to you, my God,
>> but you do not answer.
>>> I call at night, but get no rest.
> Why do you reject me, O God?
>> Why do you turn away from me?
> Ever since I was young, I have suffered and been
>> near death;
>> I am worn out from the burden of your
>> punishments.
> Your furious anger crushes me;
>> your terrible attacks destroy me.
> All day long they surround me like a flood,
>> they close in on me from every side.
> You have made even my closest friend abandon me,
>> and darkness is my only companion.
> Do not stay away from me!
>> Trouble is near, and there is no one to help.
>>>> *Psalms 22.1–2, 11; 88.14–18*[3]

The prayers which follow begin to unravel the repressed rage of the victim:

> Help me to know that anger is not a sin . . . My anger is all turned inward against myself, harming me in body and spirit. Help me to turn my anger outward, towards my abuser . . . he has sinned against me and has not kept your commandments. Call him to accountability. As he stands before you, let him know my agony and despair. Let him feel the torment of all whom he has abused.

We are ill at ease with this idea of the enemy, yet it pervades the psalms. Like the evildoers of Psalm 22 whom Jesus recalls on the cross, enemies are often real people, not just stereotypes of racism and nationalism. Our enemies may be the friend whom we trusted, the one who shared our table:

> But it was you, one after my own heart,
> my companion, my own familiar friend.
> We took sweet counsel together,
> and walked with the throng in the house of God.
> *Psalm 55.13–14 (Holy Week,* Celebrating Common Prayer)

These are chilling words when we consider how many abusers are well known family friends or people who exploit religion.

Even so, we find it hard to read the cry for revenge. We cannot easily enter into the Psalmist's apparent delight that the wicked will only be slain after they have first lost their sight and health, employment and property or that their children might be dashed against a stone (Pss. 109, 137). In our beloved Psalm 23 the enemy is made to look on while we gloat over our table of plenty. But to reject this anger outright is to deny that part of our humanity which seeks justice for those who suffer. We are pathetic creatures indeed if we have lost that instinctive revulsion to evil. From her experience of violence Sheila Cassidy found these psalms of anger a deep resource for sharing others' pain and perhaps her own.

> The power of these psalms of persecution first came to me when I was in Chile, for it is in such totalitarian states that not only are people crushed, widows, strangers and orphans killed, but their murderers parade in public . . . This rage and impotence is a deep human emotion and we do grave injustice to close our eyes to these sins that 'cry to heaven for vengeance'.[4]

Outside monastic communities, few liturgies have the stomach for this but the widely used songs from the Iona Community have brought the call for justice to more congregations.

Antiphon   *Do not keep silent, O God;*
           be neither silent nor still.
              Your enemies rise up in tumult,
              and those who hate you hold their heads high.
              They devise a cunning plot against your
                 people,
              and conspire against those whom you hold so
                 dear . . .
              Like a fire raging through the forest
              pursue your opponents with your tempest wind.
                 Psalm 83 (Psalms of Patience, Protest and Praise)

The appeal to God is not just human revenge: the sin of the unjust is fundamentally sin against God who must surely give judgment. And if there is to be real reconciliation with our enemies, we must have the courage not to sweep sin under the carpet but accept that actual people have acted with enmity towards us and others who count us as their brothers and sisters.

To avoid this also drives our resentment back into ourselves and leaves us unreconciled with God. Trying to make sense of our pain before God helps to raise us from the paralysis of depression and muster the willpower to rout our enemies outside and within.

The abandonment of God

It is their saving grace that these psalms are not merely curses but cries directed to God, putting our pain in the perspective of some greater mystery. Dietrich Bonhoeffer understood how such words could bring us closer to God by their persistent questioning:

> If I am guilty, why doesn't God forgive me? If I am inno-
> cent, why does he not end my torment and vindicate me
> before my enemies? No theoretical answer to all these
> questions is provided by the Psalms any more than by the
> New Testament. The only real answer is Jesus Christ. But
> this answer is already being sought for in the Psalms. They

are alike in casting all cares and trials upon God: we can bear them no longer, take them away and bear them yourself, only you know how to deal with suffering. That is what all the psalms of lamentation are leading up to.[5]

As we throw all this in God's face, we become aware that feeling abandoned is a reality at the heart of God. Jesus' instinctive cry from the psalms, 'My God, my God, why have you abandoned me?' brings him nearer to God than any other word could do. He might have cursed God and died but in these words he was able to own God as *his* God, pray to God, and in that prayer his cry becomes the cry of God. The reproaches of Good Friday give a haunting reflection on that desolation.

My people, what have I done to you?
How have I offended you? Answer me.

For André Néher, a French theologian of the Holocaust, the depth of God is found where the sufferer cries out by day but at night is overwhelmed by 'nonsilence' (*lo'dumiah*), 'a silence more silent than silence. It is the fall of silence into a deeper stratum of nothingness; it is a shaft hollowed out beneath silence . . . Nonsilence confronts us with a God whose Being may be grasped only from the fleeting roots of Nothingness.'[6]

I call out by day and you do not answer,
    and at night nothingness from the silence is all I have.
                                                    Psalm 22.2

This is not an absence of God's response or a rejection of us. Rather, the abandonment of the psalm draws us to the terror of divinity, the awfulness of what it is to be the Eternal one, the Maker of life and death. In our own suffering we may touch the terror of God. When the sons of Aaron are burnt by the fire of the Lord for their arrogant disobedience, Aaron is silent. Ezekiel is commanded to keep silence and not to weep when God takes away his wife, the delight of his eyes, for the destruction of God's holy temple will be just as traumatic (Lev. 10.3; Ezek. 24.15–27). Words are no help. The Jewish Mishnah tells us not to comfort people in the hour when their dead lie before them, and the suffering are exempted from saying the Shema'.[7] Silence gives us space to feel again after the numbness but in the emptiness there is an encounter with the grief of God. Paul Celan, a poet who survived persecution, speaks of that intimacy with God which only those who suffer can know:

> We are near, Lord,
> near enough for your grasp.
>
> Grasped we have been, Lord,
> clawed by one another, as though
> the body of each of us
> were your body, Lord.
>
> Pray, Lord,
> pray to us,
> we are near.
>
> *Tenebrae*

This is why the darkest places of our lives may bring us closest to God. In a comment on Psalm 139(8) Néher reminds us that 'the meeting place of God and man can be in hell'.[8] In the fearful hope that evening will cloak their guilt, Adam and Eve are sought by God. In the night of escape from cheating his brother Jacob finds a ladder to lift him from the darkness. Under the blackened sky above the crucified Jesus a soldier and a robber see God.

> Where can I go then from your spirit?
> Or where can I flee from your presence?
> If I climb up to heaven, you are there;
> if I make the grave my bed, you are there also . . .
> If I say, 'Surely the darkness will cover me,
> and the light around me turn to night',
> Even darkness is no darkness with you;
>   the night is as clear as the day;
> darkness and light to you are both alike.
>
> *Psalm 139 (Funeral Vigil,* Common Worship)

Deprived of other comfort and unable to understand the dark-

ness around us, we cannot be palmed off with easy platitudes
about providence: like Moses, we draw near to the thick darkness
where God is and in our vulnerability we are ironically better
placed to find the God who makes darkness a hiding place (Exod.
20.21; Ps. 18.11). 'This is the seeing that consists in not seeing,
because what is sought transcends all knowledge.'⁹ At rock
bottom, down there in the depths, we touch reality and touch
God. As one sufferer from depression put it:

> Unable to lift ourselves or be lifted, he stays down there
> with us in the depression – he abides in us and we in
> him . . . he does not seem to give any comfort or strength
> that one can feel consciously, but there is somehow a close-
> ness to the basic fact of things, which brings one closer to
> God.¹⁰

Suffering can only be truly redemptive when we begin to draw
God into our pain, even into our doubt and protest, for there we
shall find God sharing our grief. When Jewish teachers studied
the text 'By the waters of Babylon, there we sat; also we wept'
(Ps. 137.1), they asked what was meant by the word 'also' and
concluded that the children of Israel by their weeping caused the
Holy One, blessed be He, also to weep with them.¹¹ The depth
of God's desolation was the message given to the suffering congregation of the Warsaw Ghetto by their rabbi: God was not
hiding out of anger but because the sufferings of Israel were too
great. 'For just as God is infinite, so His pain is infinite, and this,
were it to touch the world, would destroy it.' He went on to
commend to his people a selfless solidarity, sharing God's pain.
'The pain that a person undergoes by himself alone may have the
effect of breaking him . . . but the weeping that the person does
together with God – that strengthens him.'¹² We should not be
surprised that such Jewish writers of the Holocaust offer an
insight into the passion of Jesus in whom we encounter a God
disempowered but for his tears of love. God's solidarity with us
involves suffering too awful to bear yet impossible to relinquish.
William Blake depicted this in his illustrations for the Book
of Job where God apparently turns away from Job's suffering,

but Blake perceptively gives them both the same face of abandonment.

Together in grief

To walk away from the disturbing experiences of the psalms is not only to leave ourselves unprepared if we have to face them but to neglect the pain of fellow human beings across the world in favour of a self-protecting clique without God, for we cannot have God to ourselves without his other children. 'The key to acceptance of these prayers' Sheila Cassidy says, 'lies in the Pauline concept of the Mystical Body of Christ . . . when one member is hurt, the others cry out in pain with and for him. When, therefore, we pray these psalms, we are praying not about our own pain but crying out for the persecuted.'[13]

Voice 1   I am numberless women all over the world;
          this day and every day, beaten and bloodied,
          battered and bruised by the men they live with.
Leader   Women, your home is where the hurt is:
          where shall you find refuge?
All   *Out of the depths we cry to you, O God,*
          hear our cry and listen to our prayer.
                    Women: Refuge and Adventure (Iona Community)

Praying these psalms, we face the challenge of being the people of God. Though their ritual style often casts them in the first person singular, the 'I' is all Israel, the whole Church, even if I am praying alone, for we never worship apart from the people of God and we are never separated from those who suffer. Dietrich Bonhoeffer saw that 'no single human being can pray these psalms of lamentation out of their own experience; what these psalms unfold before our eyes is the anguish of the entire community throughout all times, experienced to the uttermost by Jesus Christ alone.'[14]

The same is true of the penitential psalms. A discipline of saying these prayers, whether we feel in special need of forgiveness or not, will help us pray for and alongside those troubled by guilt. This is why a great song of confession such as Psalm 130 sets our personal need in the context of all God's people: sin has corporate consequences and forgiveness needs to be experienced in a loving community of faith. The title of the psalm, 'a song of ascents', itself suggests a pilgrim song to be prayed as we walk together.

> If you, O Lord, should mark our guilt,
> Lord, who would survive?
> But with you is found forgiveness:
> for this we revere you.
>
> My soul is waiting for the Lord,
> I count on God's word.
> My soul is longing for the Lord
> more than those who watch for
> daybreak . . .
>
> Because with the Lord there is mercy
> and fullness of redemption,
> Israel indeed God will redeem
> from all its iniquity.

Antiphon: If you, O Lord, should mark our guilt, Lord, who would survive?

(*Roman Office for the Dead*)

The stark response draws us together: we are all sinners in need of grace and we are there to watch out for each other. This is particularly reassuring when someone has died, for death rarely comes at the right time. There are words that should have been said, pain that might have been spared, kindness neglected, as well as unresolved hurt left behind by the departed. We may go on punishing ourselves with some false idea of atoning for our guilt but the Church calls on us to seek healing for living and departed alike. It is God's forgiveness not our sin that has the last word in life, as in the psalm.

Such prayer should be a continual and natural part of our worship, and not confined to the funeral itself, for it reminds us that we are on a pilgrimage of grace with all those who have gone before. In medieval times this was part of the liturgy in a more demonstrative way. At Salisbury, Sunday began with Psalm 130 chanted in procession as the canons asperged the cemetery. William Langland's working tools for ministry included the seven penitential psalms: 'with these I sing for the souls of those who help me'. This communion unbroken by death was also cherished in the earliest Christian communities of China: 'Seven times a day we praise – a great protection for the living and the dead.'[15] The theologian Catherine Pickstock sees the modern duality of life and death and the emerging individualism of religion originating in the loss of a sense of kinship between the living and the dead expressed in the medieval fraternities who prayed for the dead and founded charities in their memory. Both the living and the dead were 'involved in one unfinished story of salvation and reciprocal aid'.[16] Praying together for the departed integrates us into the community and gives us a more balanced sense of sin, not the isolated neurosis of guilt, and an objective assurance of shared forgiveness.

From the kinship of medieval society flowed the duty to give alms for the poor on behalf of the deceased. With depictions of the Last Judgment on their church walls people were less complacent about the stories Jesus told of the goats and the sheep or the rich man and Lazarus, as the haunting words of the Northumbrian Lyke-Wake Dirge reveal.

> This ae nighte, this ae nighte,
>> Every night and alle;
> Fire and fleet, and candle lighte,
>> And Christe receive thy saule . . .
> If meate or drink thou never gavest none,
>> Every night and alle;
> The fire will burn thee to the bare bone;
>> And Christ receive thy saule.

Charity did not end with death. A person's death might encourage others to found hospitals or give to the poor in their name for our forebears believed in a continuing community which, as the Body of Christ, supersedes the passing of the physical body. And, as Jesus taught, (Luke 16.9), they also understood that the deeds of the living and the departed are bound up together in the mystery of eternal salvation.

If you have shown mercy to your fellow human beings, O mortal, that same mercy shall be shown you there; and if you have shown compassion on an orphan, the same person shall deliver you there from want. If in this life you have clothed the naked, the same person shall give you shelter there, and sing the psalm, Alleluia!

(*Orthodox Burial of Priests*)

Delivery

The Psalmist affirms the power of love to liberate us even from death with a striking image. God appears as the midwife who helps to deliver us from inner darkness and total powerlessness to a new life sustained by the unbreakable bond of mother-love.

Upon you have I leaned since my birth;
from my mother's womb your strength alone brought me
out,
for you my praise shall be eternally.

Psalm 71.6 (Prayers with the dying)

It is in the Good Friday liturgy that this truth is most poignantly shown to us. As Jesus hangs on the cross, alone and apparently abandoned, his mother still stands there beside him. As he looks at her, the words of the psalm bring a bitter irony and yet also a hope in the one who can deliver us at our weakest and most vulnerable.

But it is you that took me out of the womb
and laid me safe upon my mother's breast.
On you was I cast ever since I was born;
you are my God even from my mother's womb.
Be not far from me, for trouble is near at hand,
and there is none to help.

Psalm 22.9–11 (Common Worship)

People have tended to use rebirth or birthing as a rather

comfortable image but in Hebrew Scripture the pains of labour are a metaphor for the fruitless sufferings of Israel or the judgment that God brings. It is the midwifery of God alone that can liberate us from the bondage of pain and deliver us to new life.[17] Nevertheless, we will have to cooperate. God will not let us remain just a victim.

> We have to help the victim to stand up and work with God and others for better ways in relationships. We have to help the victim-self to have the courage to question and get into dialogue with the internal critic, the put-down oppressor, who casts an idolatrous shadow over how we experience God, whose love is without limits.[18]

Yet the midwife image makes it clear that we are not alone. 'No one was born alone. To be born presupposes relationship, connection, community.'[19] The God who delivers me from the womb and lays me on my mother's breast is an ikon of what the liberating community of faith should be.

And this is the strength of the psalms. They express our deepest feelings for which no ordinary language is adequate and yet we are in company with others in great need who wrote and sang them. With them our emotions are held yet released in a rhythm which channels them into healing and all this within the worshipping body of the Church where we see our grief with a larger vision than private tears could ever give us. The Russian theologian Pavel Florensky, who ended his days in a Stalinist labour camp, described how in worship

> Cult weeps with us, for us, it speaks words which are exactly what we would want to say but would never be able to say. In short, to our dim individual grief, to our chaotic, accidentally shaped, and perhaps, in our minds, even illicit grief, it gives universal form, the form of pure humanity. Cult raises grief in us, and thereby raises us in our grief, to the level of ideal humanity, to that very human nature created in the likeness of Christ.[20]

Part of that transformation from private to universal comes from the music. Reciting, and better singing, is a physical activity that draws the breath of our whole body from aimlessness and exhaustion to a rhythm and energy. I have even known people benefit from reciting the psalms when suffering from hyperventilation for their poetry restores equilibrium and helps us take body and soul again into our own hands.

Light in darkness

Whether we express it as the powerless dependency of the womb or the unfathomable depths swept by raging elements above us, we come to know, as we worship with God's people, that in the darkness light may be found. One of the most dramatic examples of this illumination comes in the Orthodox Vespers of Good Friday. We have just lamented the hanging of a good man on the tree. The invisible One is overcome, the Redeemer is bound in the prison of the grave. Then we hear this astonishing contrast at the evening lighting of the lamps:

> O gladdening Light of the Father's holy glory,
> immortal, heavenly, holy, blessed, Jesus Christ,
> as we have come to the setting of the sun,
> we see the evening light,
> and we sing to God, Father, Son, and Holy Spirit.
> It is right to sing to you at every time
> with voices of praise, O son of God, Giver of Life:
> therefore, the world gives you glory!

> *Prokimenon (Psalms 22.18, 1* Gk)
> They parted my garments among them,
> and for my vestment they cast lots.
> V   *O God, my God, come to my help:*
>   *why have you forsaken me?*

The insight in this hymn that we see the light as darkness falls is ultimately reflected in the Passion of Christ where the darkness which encompasses the death of the Son of God becomes the dawn of new life. God alone can take our pain, even our cries of abandonment or revenge, and illuminate them with life-giving grace. Our inner darkness must have a part, perhaps a necessary

part, in God's redemptive purpose so that we may even ask
with Hildegard, 'How could light be recognized except through
darkness?' and conclude that 'the part full of darkness with its
empty space serves the part which is light.'[21] In our anger and
self-pity, when we think we have withdrawn into a hidden world
of our own, 'even the remotest and most inaccessible caverns of
the heart turn out to be occupied already, and the darkness in
which the person had hoped to save their personal existence
from annihilation in Being is already ablaze with the glory of
God.'[22]

Such assurance does not come to order just when we need it.
'We must extinguish the candle, put out the light and relight
it, forever must quench, forever relight the flame.'[23] Faith grows
through our spiritual journey, nurtured by Word, sacrament and
the kindness of others. The Psalter is a pilgrim book whose
meanings unfold the more we travel with it. It carries the presence and power of God, contradicting every evidence of grief
around us, taking us through the landscape of our sorrow and
giving us a horizon where we could see none, even filling the
emptiness of a mourner's house with light.

> The Lord is my light and my salvation,
>   whom then shall I fear? . . .
> Wait for the Lord, be strong and let your heart take
>   courage:
> yes, wait I say, for the Lord.
> *The minister may stand beside the body and say*
> We commend . . . to God, as s/he journeys beyond
>   our sight.
> God of all consolation, in your unending love and
>   mercy
> you turn the darkness of death into the dawn of new
>   life . . .
>
>   *Psalm 27 (Prayers before a Funeral,*
>   A New Zealand Prayer Book)

The hope is no illusion: God's light confronts our real darkness
and engages with the human wickedness which we are too weak
to fight. And just when we think that we shall not come through,

the Psalmist reminds us that the future of God's people rested on an improbable promise to a small tribal leader that his descendants would be as numerous as the sand on the seashore. (Gen. 22.17).

> How precious to me are Your thoughts, O God!
> How vast is their number!
> Were I to count them,
> they would outnumber the grains of the sand.
> Were I to finish the count,
> I would still be with You.
> If only You would slay the wicked, O God!
> Away from me, you bloodthirsty men!
> *Psalm 139.17–19 (Prayer to be said by a sick person*, ADPB)

The promise is that when we have come to the end, when we finish the count of mortal days, we are still in God's realm. The psalm ends with this eschatological note, asking God to guide us in the everlasting way, but today and eternity cannot be separated in Hebrew thought. As Herbert Levine comments, this way 'as this psalmist certainly knows, is not a path human beings can literally walk in this lifetime. What the psalmist holds out by means of this figurative expression is the hope of walking in partnership with God towards ends within this lifetime, such as justice and righteous living, that God has taught are endless.'[24] The walk that transcends death begins here and the eternal Light of God is already illuminating our darkness within and guiding us on.

> Search me out, O God, and know my heart:
> try me and know my restless thoughts.
> Look well whether there be any wickedness in me:
> and lead me in the way that is everlasting.
> *Psalm 139.23–4 (Evening Prayer for the Departed*,
> Celebrating Common Prayer)

EIGHT

The Lord of the Dance

Remembering the way

Has God forgotten to be gracious
and in anger shut up the womb of his love? . . .
I will remember the works of the Lord,
for I will remember your wonders of old . . .
Your way was through the sea
and your paths through the mighty waters,
but your footprints were not known.

Psalm 77.9, 11, 19

Remembering in Hebrew religion is not nostalgia for the past, even the religious past. The Psalmist searches for help now. Once the waters of the Red Sea fled before the divine presence at the Exodus. God's footsteps were not seen then and they are as hard to imagine in our own trials, but in our deepest need, obscured by our imminent fears and despair, the unseen, the unthinkable, can be reality.

This remembering does not try to recreate the past. It is the shared memory of how God has guided people and fulfilled a purpose through them. The Western linear model of memory with its regret or ambition has no place. This is a different concept of time rooted in history but lived in experience. Traditional African spirituality has a similar perspective: 'When you speak of time, you actually speak of people, ie. the relationship of past, present and future generations . . . For the African, the present is in the future and the future is in the present.'[1]

So also for Jews. At the beginning of the Passover meal, the youngest at table asks what this night is all about, immediately bonding the generations. Later, the leader affirms that 'in every generation each human being should see that in their very bones they too came out of Egypt . . . for the Holy One, blessed be He, did not only redeem our forebears alone, but redeemed us with them.' Psalm 118 was probably written for the autumn New Year festival but, as the last of the Hallel psalms sung at Passover, it carries with it the joy of God's deliverance at the Exodus. Before the destruction of the Temple, these psalms were recited with special music as the Passover lamb was sacrificed and the congregation would respond loud and often. Likewise today at Passover, each of the first four lines of Psalm 118 is repeated:

> Give thanks to the Lord who is good:
> > *for God's love is for ever.*
> Let Israel now say:
> > *for God's love is for ever.*
> Let the house of Aaron now say:
> > *for God's love is for ever.*
> Let those who fear the Lord now say:
> > *for God's love is for ever.*

The repetition of verses already containing a response broadcasts universal salvation shared across the ages. The God who has rescued and raised up the oppressed in the past will faithfully do the same for us.

A fool for God

We are also taken across the threshold of past generations into the age to come. At the Passover meal, after the third cup of wine is drunk 'to peace', the cups are refilled and the door is opened for the coming of Elijah, the forerunner of the Messiah. Against the draught of the outside world prayers are said for the defeat of Israel's enemies. An additional goblet of wine stands filled for the prophet. With this background of Messianic hope the Hallel psalms are recited before the fourth and final cup is drunk, symbolic of the fulfilment of the promises represented in the four letters of the unspoken name of God, YHWH. Psalm 118 itself focuses on the Anointed One who comes in the name of the Lord, for the king's special association with the power of the divine name indicates an intimate personal relationship with God (Ps. 118, 10–12, 26, 28 *cf.* Ps. 89.26). The ritual setting here also involves signs of the Messiah, the enactment of a struggle against enemies and a triumphal entry into the Temple.

For, personal though this relationship with God was, the king inherited a long tradition of responsibility for the whole people. We find Abraham pleading for the people of Sodom, bound to plead even for the sake of ten righteous people. Moses tells Israel frankly that he bears the anger of the Lord for their sins and even intercedes for them, asking God to blot him out of the book of life if their sins may not be forgiven. In the Temple liturgy the Psalmist bids God to remember David's ordeal as a blessing for the nation and the heart of Solomon's prayer of consecration is that God will hear and forgive (Gen. 18.22–3; Deut. 3.26; 4.21; Exod. 32.32; Ps. 132; 1 Kings 8). The king apparently wore on his turban a golden flower, found on Judean jar stamps, which had an atoning significance.[2] Ezekiel envisaged that, after the Exile, the royal leader would again provide sin-offerings for the atonement of Israel (Ezek. 45.17). Even the cleansing image of pounding dirt from clothes may have been a ritual scourging and sprinkling of the king performed on behalf of all (Ps. 51.2, 7).[3] The obedience of the Lord's Anointed is held to be of far more importance to God and the congregation than perfunctory sacrifices and the tears of his laments are kept in God's record as a source of thanksgiving and renewal for the future (*cf.* Pss. 40.6–10; 56).

In our Passover psalm the king immediately proceeds to tell of his own ordeal but it is a ritual that gathers up a whole people's trauma.

> Out of my dire straits I called on the Lord,
> who answered me with great freedom . . .
> All the ungodly hemmed me in:
> by the name of the Lord I drove them back.
> They hemmed me in, they hemmed me in:

by the name of the Lord I drove them back.
They hemmed me in like bees, blazing like a fire of thorns:
by the name of the Lord I drove them back.

Psalm 118.5, 10–12

The Hebrew word for 'straits' *(metsar)* suggests a narrow and dangerous place, indeed the straits of death (Pss. 116; 18.4–6). The fourfold attack from the heathen nations presses in upon the king so as to make him fall. This is no personal tragedy: he represents a holy people against a violent and unbelieving world. Elsewhere, the king appears in sackcloth, fasting, as he undergoes this crisis but the Lord hears his cry (Pss. 3.4; 18.6; 69.10–11). The place of this struggle is described as a pit with water and slippery rocks (Pss. 9.15; 18.16–19; 69.1–2) such as Gihon, the Temple spring, with its appropriately cosmic associations. The scourging is seen not as an accident of history but as the work of God, a deliberate confrontation with evil, possibly ritualized in a threefold attack by prophets assailing the Anointed One in the subterranean darkness (*cf.* Ps. 73.14).

The Hebrew text (usually altered) dramatizes the conflict. As the king recounts his struggle, he suddenly turns and challenges his enemies to their face:

They came about me like bees . . .
Thou hast thrust sore at me, that I might fall:
but the Lord was my help.

Psalm 118.12–13 (BCP)⁺

We have to face up to the threat of evil which undermines our belief in an omnipotent and faithful God. The problem is as much ours as the Psalmist's. Left unchallenged, evil can destroy the rationale and integrity of worship and, with it, the fabric of our community. Israel hardly needed real enemies to know this: history provided enough external dangers and internal corruption for this never to have been an academic discussion. Her prophets were not afraid to confront her painful memories in this way. The psalms are a testimony that pain remembered and encountered before God can be changed from hurt to praise in the liturgy.

The very recital permits a rereading of trouble that ends in the glad practice of praise . . . The trouble has been set in the context of remembered praise. But conversely the present pain also keeps the act of praise honest . . . The present reality of pain within which praise is done reminds Israel that this longstanding formulation of praise was articulated and utilized precisely in a context of pain . . . As praise recontextualizes pain, so pain refocuses praise.[5]

Such a song of faith, wrung out of many remembered conflicts, is itself a triumph. The salvation proclaimed by the Psalmist was probably symbolized by clothing the sovereign in royal robes (*cf.* Ps. 132.16) but the reference to song should not be overlooked. The testimony of praise contrasts with wild taunts which resembled the buzzing of bees against the clear voice of human faith. Music has a force in itself for the chants of our forebears' faith become a confirmation of our own, however weak, and a defiant proclamation to the world. In the Nazi Holocaust Jews went to their death, challenging their enemy and their own humiliation as they sang, 'I believe with perfect faith in the coming of the Messiah – and though he tarry, I still believe.' Sustaining the song of faith is a proof that God has vindicated us. 'The Lord is my strength and my song.'

As the king processes in our psalm to the Temple gate, he comes with the authority of a vocation tested and proved by God and boldly claims entry to the holy place whose congregation will publicly affirm that he is God's chosen one.

> Open to me the gates of righteousness,
> that I may enter and give thanks to the Lord.
> This is the gate of the Lord:
> the righteous shall enter through it.
> I will give thanks to you, for you have answered me
> and have become my salvation.
> *Psalm 118.19–23 (Easter Gradual*, Common Worship)

To have that special relationship of sonship with God like the king, to know that you have been marked out and guided, meant being open to pain and struggling with all the loneliness peculiar to leadership and the apparent folly of its calling. We read it in the story of David himself. He feigns madness to fool King Achish, scratching the doors of the gate and letting spittle run down his beard. He is not afraid to dance before the Ark of the Lord, rejecting Michal's jealousy and telling her that he is ready to make himself 'yet more contemptible than this'. He shows his spiritual strength in public by weeping and fasting for his own sins or for his treacherous son, even at the cost of shaming his victorious army and embarrassing his political advisers (1 Sam. 21.12–15; 2 Sam. 6.12–22; 2 Sam. 12.15–17; 2 Sam 19.1–8). Jesus cites David's unconventional conduct when defending his own ministry (Mark 2.23–8).

God's Anointed was to show Israel how she, like him, could pass through suffering and universal derision and still fulfil a priestly role for the world. The figure of the fool has been exemplified in Christian tradition by saints like Mark the Mad, Moling, Ramon Lull, Symeon of Emesa, Isaac of Kiev and notably Francis of Assisi. The painter Cecil Collins has given us a more coherent theology of this spirituality: he saw that the fool's freedom comes from paying no heed to status or power. He cannot be exploited because he is of no practical use, challenging a utilitarian society with longings of the spirit which the world cannot manipulate. Worse still, the fool awakens the fool in others. 'The true priest is a Fool whose purity of spirit is the folly by which the world grows and becomes enlightened.' So Collins could draw Christ as the Fool, helplessly bound at his trial yet ignoring the aggressive might of Pilate as if it were irrelevant. On the cross, he depicts Christ looking graciously upon a parade of dancing troubadors who come to comfort him while he turns away from a rigid line of oppressive figures, wearing helmets like a bishop's mitre![6] His damning indictment of the Church is that it has compromised with the spirit of the age, abandoning the values of divine folly and the call to humiliation. 'No one would think to crucify the Church; there is nothing to crucify.'[7]

The fascination of fools and the reason for their rejection are the otherness they bring to life. With Israel's monarch we might imagine this to be an aura cultivated to protect status. With Jesus people thought it arrogance or eccentricity. But this otherness is not exclusive: it draws us to a secret about ourselves. 'Other, but never a stranger, Other, deeper within me than my inmost depths . . . The Altogether Other is Altogether Near. It is also because he is other than man, that Christ is incomparably close.'[8] In the psalms, the otherness of the sovereign comes not from status, political skill or military power but from the continued guidance of God, who alone is strength and salvation.

The stone that moved, the day that lasts for ever

The lasting effects of God's saving work for the whole community around the king are shown in the paradox of two images in Psalm 118: the stone and the day.

> The Lord's right hand has triumphed;
> God's right hand raised me.
> I shall not die, I shall live
> and recount God's deeds.
>
> The stone which the builders rejected
> has become the corner stone.
> This is the work of the Lord,
> a marvel in our eyes.
> > *This day was made by the Lord;*
> > *we rejoice and are glad.*
> > Psalm 118.16–17, 22–4 (Easter Gradual, Roman Rite)

The word 'cornerstone' (*pinnah*) is sometimes derived from the verb 'to turn' and certainly the path of the Lord's Anointed turns at this point in the ritual procession of the psalm. The stone, rejected by the world, has proved its pivotal strength, holding together the gateway to life. Here also is a memory of Passover. From the rock God nourished the people in the wilderness with water, honey and oil, nursing them like a mother-eagle and Jewish legend speaks of Miriam's well within the rock following them through the desert (Deut. 32 *cf.* 1 Cor. 10.4; Pss. 81.16; 105.41).

The stone that is rejected confirms for Jesus the integrity of

his own journey as he confronts the models of power represented
by the leaders of the day. The shouts of Hosanna from the same
psalm echo about him but he finds strength in rediscovering
the Messianic tradition of redemption through rejection (Mark
12.10–11; Matt. 21.42). The Early Church took up the theology
of the cornerstone in its apostolic preaching of Jesus as the
source of life for the deprived and the foundation for the
worshipping community of living stones offering spiritual sacrifices on behalf of the world (Acts 4.11; 1 Pet. 2.7).

The strength and nourishment of the rock may explain its
inclusion at the offertory in the Liturgy of St James used in Syrian
churches such as the Mar Thoma:

> You, O Lord, are the rock whence water flowed
> for the children of Israel;
> You are the precious stone which the builders rejected.

In the West, this guiding image appears in the desert journeyings
of Advent and Lent. The antiphon 'O King of the nations'
celebrates the 'cornerstone who makes all one' while the Advent
Prose prays God to 'send forth the Lamb, the ruler of the earth,
from the desert rock to the mount of daughter Zion' – a phrase
usually omitted in English translations. The Lent Prose finds
consolation in the chief Cornerstone who is also Way of Salvation
and Gate of Life celestial.

Just as the stone travels, the image of the day is unlimited.
Worship before God on any day moves us into the sacred time
and space of eternity. This is not some imaginary world escaping
the course of real events: worshippers 'accept the present
moment as a unique gift from the Father, as the very will of God
for them now, as the point where they meet their eternal bliss.[9]
For prophets like Zephaniah the day of the Lord was not a parable
or distant vision. It was a ritual of sacrifice, bringing a renewal of
the covenant with joy for the faithful, encompassing the disabled
and the outcast, but for idolaters and corrupt traders of the
Second Quarter of the city it would be a day of judgment and
ruin. The hours of a day may be limited but the work of God on
a day has eternal consequences not in future ages alone but in the
local neighbourhood now (Zeph. 1.7–13). The redemption of

Passover takes us to a shore by the Red Sea. The Christian Pass-over occurs on a hill and in a garden of Jerusalem on the first day of the week. George Herbert captures the paradox of the day which is specific and destined to pass yet lasts for ever:

> Can there be any day but this,
> Though many sunnes to shine endeavour?
> We count three hundred, but we misse:
> There is but one, and that one ever.

Easter

Lord of fire and light

The Lord's Anointed has been vindicated through humiliating trials, clothed in the garments of salvation, and enters the sanctuary. Now the fruits of this Messianic struggle are revealed and the congregation cry out:

> *'Anna 'Adonai hoshi 'ah nna*
> Now, Lord, save us, we pray!
> Now, Lord, make us prosper, we pray!

Psalm 118.25

During these words at the Feast of Tabernacles (Sukkot), water was poured over the altar and the earth beside it was beaten with willow branches called Hoshanot. The way this psalm has been used for the Sabbath also suggests an ancient ritual of prayer for rain.[10] It was understood that the welfare of the king brought blessing on all. When David brings the Ark of the Lord back into the Temple, bread for the poor and provisions for the people flow from his obedient priesthood (Ps. 132). The ritual battle of Psalm 144 concludes with the sovereign's triumphant prayer for new generations of sons and daughters for Israel, full barns, prosperous flocks and security for the community. Even after the most traumatic rejection of Psalm 22, the deliverance of God's chosen one means that the afflicted can now eat and be satisfied and all the families of the nations will acknowledge the Lord. The promise is taken up by the risen Christ who uses the Psalmist's words to commission

Mary to 'go and tell my brothers' (John 20.17; Heb. 2.12; *cf.* Ps. 22.22). The ikon of God's anointed king and priest in Psalm 110 depicts him shining with the dew of fresh oil and being revived after the conflict with running water. In Paul it becomes a prophecy of Christ's victory, bringing the fruits of resurrection to the baptized (1 Cor. 15.20–9).

With the water of life comes the light. The feast of Tabernacles was celebrated with torchlight dances and it was said that whoever had not seen its joy had never seen joy in all their life.[11] The Psalmist describes a joyful procession of light in which the people felt a part. We do not watch the glory of God as spectators without becoming part of what we see. Through Scripture, music and prayer, God does appear among this people at prayer. For Irenaeus, this spiritual illumination could be described with the same language of partaking as communion.

> Just as those who see the light are within the light, and partake of its brightness, so those who see God are within God, partaking of God's brightness. But God's brightness makes them come alive: those who see God, therefore, partake of life.[12]

In the Syrian churches of India, worshippers may be seen both offering gifts of oil to the central oil lamp and anointing themselves with the oil for blessing and healing, physically partaking of the light.

The Eucharist is the tryst where the liturgy not only indicates but reveals the light in the real presence of the risen Christ, light which transfigures us in communion. In the Liturgy of St John Chrysostom the consecrated bread and wine are shown to the congregation as they are invited to communion with the words:

> Blessed is the one coming in the name of the Lord.
> The Lord is God who has shone light upon us.
>
> *Psalm 118.26–7*

In ancient Israel and Orthodoxy alike, the context shows that light is not a static image in psalmody. Light, often in the dynamic form of fire, is the clothing of the Lord who comes to rescue the oppressed and destroy evil and whose presence is revealed in the offering of burning sacrifices. In the Temple Isaiah sees the glory of the Lord but his lips are touched with a coal of fire. Enslaved in Babylon, Ezekiel sees the cloud of God's glory flashing with fire. The torchlight procession of our psalm recalls the Passover path of God's people, travelling through the wilderness with the guiding pillar of cloud and fire, the divine presence which burns their idols and descends in flames upon Mount Sinai to send them on their journey with the Law. The Psalmist envisages the Lord riding upon the cherubim, heralded by fire melting the mountains, setting forests ablaze with lightning, consuming the enemy, but bringing light and joy to the righteous and keeping faith with God's chosen one (Pss. 18, 29, 97, 99).

Apart from the new fire of the Easter Vigil, this is an image yet to be explored in liturgy, though hymn writers like Ephrem, Symeon the New Theologian and the Wesleys have used it to convey the awesome union of opposites, human and divine, which is forged in the mystery of communion.[13] A recovery of incense in worship would help us recover a more dynamic view of the God who comes to abide among us and within us. In many churches, the practice of kindling the light at evening prayer has been restored and the accompanying prayers can facet enriching images from the history of salvation.

> Blessed are you, Sovereign God,
> our light and our salvation;
> to you be glory and praise for ever!
> You led your people to freedom
> by a pillar of cloud by day
> and a pillar of fire by night.
> May we who walk in the light of your presence
> acclaim your Christ, rising victorious,
> as he banishes all darkness from our hearts and minds,
> and praise you, Father, Son, and Holy Spirit;
> *Blessed be God for ever!*
> *Sunday Evening Prayer* (Celebrating Common Prayer)

Of all the psalms celebrating God's coming in fire Psalm 68, often appropriately used for Pentecost, most powerfully portrays the God of the Exodus, the God of Sinai, gathering up the wandering tribes, forging a people under the Law and sending them on a journey of promise, their way lit by the presence of the God who travels with them.

> Rise, O God, defend the right,
> Let your enemies take flight.
> Come as wind and cleansing flame,
> Joy to all who praise your name!
>
> Come as guardian of the poor,
> Home for wanderers at your door;
> Here you grant the lonely peace,
> Guiding prisoners to release.
>
> Through the wilderness you lead,
> Sheltering your flock in need.
> Earth reveres your presence, Lord,
> Showering plenteous rain abroad.
>
> Now the Lord has given the word;
> Women, let the news be heard.
> Rebel hearts God reigns above,
> Gathering from us gifts of love.
>
> Every congregation, sing!
> See the coming of our King;
> Welcomed to this holy place,
> Drums and singers sound your grace.
>
> Peoples of the world, reply:
> Sing to God who rides the sky.
> Bless the Lord whose mighty voice
> Gives us courage to rejoice!

Pentecost Processional (*Tune:* Orientis Partibus)

The cosmic dance

The procession of Psalm 68 is led by singers, followed by girls playing tambourines and other musicians, but they are 'processions of my God, my King, into the sanctuary', with the divine power symbolized by the Ark of the Law which was usually carried to the accompaniment of drums, shakers, cymbals and dancing (2 Sam. 6). Dance had always captured the joy of God's mighty acts. Women like Miriam and Judith were among its leaders (Exod. 15.20–1; Judith 15.12–18). The people of God did not wander aimlessly through life: as they moved into the Temple so they moved through life, joyfully and purposefully for God went with them.

A similar drama unfolds in Psalm 118 as the procession, led by the victorious king, comes into the sanctuary.

> Join the festal dance with green branches
> up to the horns of the altar.

Psalm 118.27

The word for festival procession or dance here (*hag cf.* the Islamic Haj at Mecca) indicates a liturgical dance encircling the altar, celebrating the commitment and saving grace which God and the people of the Covenant share and perhaps acting as a ritual protection against hostile forces. It marks out sacred space and a sense of belonging in that space. Ritual has a valuable role in helping us cross that immeasurable distance between the holy and mysterious ways of the divine and our need to know God close at hand. The procession of people into the Temple sanctuary, like the walk of communicants to the altar, drew them across the threshold of doubt and failure into closer communion with God. The sacrificial system itself had this effect. Sacrifices for sins unwarily committed were offered outside in the courtyard while the most wanton communal sins could only receive atonement when the high priest took the blood of the sacrifice right into the holy of holies.

The processional dance around the altar marks a turning point not just for the worshippers but for the world, for the people bring with them symbols of creation: leafy branches which will be tied to the altar itself. From this womb of the Temple and navel of the earth, the life-giving power of God will renew the whole creation and bind it to God's purposes as the people have bound themselves in this ritual. Rowan Williams has argued how for Christians also the ritual of the sacraments makes us re-evaluate our present condition and leads us to abandon secular concepts of power and status of human choosing for God's new community of interdependence:

> The sacramental action . . . tells us that where we habitu-ally are is not, after all, a neutral place but a place of loss or need. It then requires us to set aside this damaged or needy condition, this flawed identity, so that in dispossessing our-selves of it we are able to become possessed of a different identity, given in the rite, not constructed by negotiation and co-operation like other kinds of social identity. The rite requires us not to belong any more to the categories we thought we belonged in, so that a distinctive kind of new belonging can be realized.[14]

This new commitment in our psalm is expressed with a vow of thanks and loyalty, which, according to the great biblical commentator Abraham Ibn Ezra, represents the response of each pilgrim at the feast:

> You are my God and I will thank you,
> my God, I will raise your praises high.
>
> *Psalm 118.28*

All that has been remembered, experienced, re-discovered is now owned by each worshipper as their own story. The suffering of God's Anointed and his vindicated faith are not a pageant for royalty but a sacrament of liberation for all to share. The worshippers not only told the story: they were the ongoing story. 'Liturgy does not merely commemorate an event. It *is* that event, and the event is the person or persons that enacts or enact the same archetypal ritual in a time that is essentially their time.'[15]

This dynamic view of remembering has involved Christians in marking out a sacred space and identifying themselves as heirs of its story. The first Christians would gather at the very sites where martyrs, 'dancers of the Holy Spirit' as they were called, had suffered. 'The community of Antioch not only danced in the churches and in the oratories of the martyrs but proclaimed the victory of the cross even in the theatres.'[16] In the West, the thirteenth-century ring-dance or carol took up the joy of Christmas, often re-living the journey of shepherds and wise men to the manger and inviting us to travel with them into eternity:

> Leve we al this werdly merthe,
> And folwe we this joyful berthe; Transeamus.
>
> *'There is no rose' (c. 1450)*

Processions celebrate our part in the victory and resurrection of Christ, whether to the Easter Garden as a promise of paradise restored or to the waters of baptism with the new light of the Paschal candle. The psalmody of the Exodus experience continues to express the new realm into which we have entered.

> The stone the builders rejected
> R　*Has become the cornerstone.*
> The Lord is God
> R　*And has shown us light.*
> Join the dance, bring fresh greenery for the feast:
> R　*Come and dance your way to the altar.*
>
> *Psalm 118 (The Blessing of the Easter Garden)*

> Great things the Lord has done for us:
> R　*And we are glad indeed.*
> Turn us, Lord, to you to find new life,
> R　*Like streams of water on dry ground.*
> Those who sow in tears
> R　*Shall reap with shouts of joy.*
>
> *Psalm 126 (The Blessing of the Easter Garden)*

Like the people of the Exodus or the humbled king, God turns our steps in a radically different direction from human ambitions of power and greed to a new world recreated by divine grace. Easter Vespers is another occasion for remembering this way of our calling. In medieval Salisbury, as in many other places, at the

close of Easter Day the clergy and people processed with oil and
chrism to the font. The change of lifestyle and destiny symbolized in baptism was expressed in this communal walk to the font
and the accompanying psalm praises the God who reverses the
plight of human frailty and injustice.

> Alleluia, praise the Lord, you children of God:
>> praise the Name of the Lord. Alleluia! . . .
> Who is like the Lord our God, who dwells on high,
>> yet looks to what is lowly in heaven and on earth?
>>> Alleluia!
> Lifting up the needy from the ground
>> and raising the poor from the dung heap. Alleluia!
> To gather them together with the princes,
>> the princes of God's people. Alleluia!
>
> *Psalm 113.1–3, 5–8*[17]

Eternity rubs shoulders with the here and now. Easter is
marked by the sun rising and setting, and yet it is a day for ever,
overturning all the world's values and priorities. The once-for-all
lowering into the baptismal waters and raising up from the font
means that God is continually raising the needy and working out
the mystery of salvation in us.

Shelter for the journey

The procession of Psalm 118 ends at the altar, whose sacred
space demonstrated the protection and sanctuary God offers the
people of the covenant. In the psalms it is often described by
the image of the *sukkāh*, a hut woven with branches to shelter
farmers in their fields at harvest time, which later became a
symbol of Israel's nomadic years in the wilderness commemorated at the Feast of Sukkot. Then the people would carry citrus
fruit (*'etrog*) and palms entwined with myrtle and willow (*lulav*)
and wave them in procession (*cf.* Lev. 23.40). The leafy branches
in Psalm 118 may well refer to such a ritual and the procession
to the altar exults in the house of God whose gates betoken safety
and salvation for the righteous. Herbert Levine has revealed the

significance of this metaphor for Israel, as they came out of alienation from God into communion with God:

> We might say that in the midst of their disorientation, psalmists reorient themselves to believe in the power of a saving God by envisioning themselves hiding within God's presence, in the image of a concealing, sheltering *sukkāh*. The metaphor allows psalmists to express conflicting, even paradoxical, emotions. They sorely feel their vulnerability in a world where God's justice often seems to be hidden, so they focus on their need to feel especially sheltered, in fact, treasured, by a sheltering God, whose special intimacy is available to them through worship in God's sanctuary.[18]

The metaphor may have been actually visible in the sanctuary if, as some think, the Ark was surrounded by a *sukkāh*, conveying, like the covering wings of the cherubim, both the intimacy and awe of God's protection and communion. For the Psalmist, the beauty of God's house seems to rest in the fact that it is a place of refuge, contemplation and communion:

> There is one thing I ask of the Lord,
> for this I long,
> to live in the house of the Lord,
> all the days of my life,
> to savour the sweetness of the Lord,
> to behold his temple.
> For God makes me safe in his tent [*besukkoh*]
> in the day of evil.
> God hides me in the shelter of his tent,
> on a rock I am secure.
>
> *Psalm 27.4–5 (Evening Prayer, Roman Rite)*

This sense of sanctuary and security in the psalms is valued by many at night, when the quiet of the hour allows worries to surface and our restlessness is most at odds with our need to sleep. God's sheltering presence in this Jewish night prayer reassures us, even as the dying Jesus turned to its words for strength (Luke 23.46).

How great and plenteous is your goodness, Lord,
which you have kept hidden for those who revere you . . .
you will protect them in a shelter [*besukkoh*] from the strife
   of tongues.

Psalm 31.19–20 (Orthodox Great Compline)

The shelter of the sanctuary should not be thought of as a
dream of ultimate solitude; it is central to the political and
liturgical life of the community. And we must remember that the
sukkah is an interim dwelling for a vulnerable in-between time,
agriculturally between the growing and rainy seasons when
harvest hangs in the balance, historically in the wilderness
between slavery and the promised land.[19] The procession to the
altar tells us that we are a people in transition, on the move.

NINE

A Taste of Paradise

Nourishment or negation

> Have you never noticed how keenly little children will
> sometimes cling to their mother's breasts when they are
> hungry? . . . But, after the freshness of the milk has allayed
> the heat of their stomach and the delightful vapours which
> it sends begin to lull them to sleep, you will see them softly
> shut their eyes and little by little give way to sleep, yet
> without letting go of the breast . . . for, if one draws the
> breast away from them before they fall asleep, they awake
> and cry, showing by their sorrow how great their content-
> ment was, when they possessed their mother.[1]

Taste is not a luxury; it is a matter of staying alive. Survival
depends on our senses. As soon as we are born, the waiting
world greets our first cry with joy and relief, assured that we can
breathe and begin our own battle for life. In that cry, too, people
know that we can communicate, as we shall need to, for the
word is life to us.

Hunger and thirst bring us to our mother's breast. And from
Isaiah's picture of God as mother to the apostles' bidding to suck
the pure milk of Christ's Gospel, the people of God have found
the first taste of life a wonder comparable with our relationship
with God (Isa. 66.10–13; 1 Cor. 3.1–2; 1 Pet. 2.2). For, as with
the rest of the animal kingdom, taste and touch, smell and sight
and hearing, are more than sources of pleasure and nourishment
for the body or signals of warning in times of danger. Once a

new individual is born and physically separated from the mother, taste begins to communicate love and warmth, bonding parent and baby together. Many spiritual writers have pointed out that the breast lies close to the heart.

Christians have not always looked at the physical world so positively. In the New Testament swollen rivers and stormy seas are either a threat to the apostles' mission or a metaphor for vacillation. The animal world is represented by oxen treading out the grain and horses that must be bridled. Human art and craft are functional: Saul's tentmaking and Lydia's trade with purple cloth indicate their livelihood, not artistic beauty. It is true that when Paul looks for a symbol for the indescribable miracle of the resurrection, he does turn to the glory of sun, moon and stars and he accords some 'weaker' yet indispensable parts of the body more honour, but even this distinction reveals a basic ambiguity about the physical world. The body is the temple of the Holy Spirit but we are to subdue it, pummel it and finally crucify it![2]

For writers such as Paul, their age of persecution left no room for an aesthetic appreciation of creation, which for them was groaning in labour for liberation. The exception, the Apocalypse, depicts not the beauty of the present world, brutalized by inhumanity, but a new heaven and a new earth in eternity.

This ambivalence to the physical has poisoned much of our Christian tradition. Where the material is not actually rejected as evil, it has been often felt that it must be controlled. And women, sometimes regarded as more in touch with the physical realm, have been particular victims of this dualism. Tertullian, for example, regarded woman as a sword against the man, even if she was blameless, for her beauty undermined male self-control; his jealousy was her fault. Augustine thought sex was inherently lustful, because it induced a state where passion overwhelmed reason, as if the touchstone of religion were mastery rather than mystery. In this arena of male pathology the physical world existed only to be analysed and controlled. Its function was to inform us of God's natural law. So Luther's observations of animal behaviour led him to conclude from the food chain that everything in turn becomes filth.[3]

Our own idolatry of market forces has led us down a similarly barren road of ravished rain forests, an irreparably damaged ozone layer, and the dignity of workers sacrificed for profit. We have been conditioned by packaged food and culture and have diluted the raw colour and excitement of nature. In a world of plastic imitation, tastes quickly satisfied, video and computer to analyse and control what we sense, in a church culture of tame sermons and predictable songs, we have excluded the surprise of the unexpected and made creation into a parody, instantly accessible and saleable.

Though this distorted view has scarred the Church, it has never quite won, for at the centre of our faith the human body itself is taken by God, the Word made flesh, who redeemed the world in his own body and rose from the dead so that we could proclaim, 'I believe in the resurrection of the flesh', to put the Latin literally. It has never won because Jesus is a Jew who believes God saw what was created and it was good. For his birth the earth provides a cave, according to Eastern tradition. He can be at peace while the storms of Lake Galilee terrify his followers. He seems to know how to work with the elements, even teaching fishermen where to cast their nets. He sees that cornfields which can feed the hungry are part of the holiness of the Sabbath. For Jesus the wonder of a fragile world is not in its function but in the beauty with which the Creator clothes it, a beauty far beyond human endeavour.

> Consider the lilies of the field, how they grow;
> they neither toil nor spin;
> yet I tell you, even Solomon in all his glory
> was not arrayed like one of these.
>
> *Matthew 6.28–9*

Jesus also points to the rhythm of the seasons to demonstrate God's purpose. The buds on the trees as summer approaches are a parable for the nearness of the kingdom; the widely scattered seed and the mustard-tree sheltering all the birds of heaven indicate divine inclusiveness. The carefully tended vine and its life-giving sap represent Jesus' own offering of life.

In his world the material is where we encounter God. The Jordan's water is the element in which people find renewal.

Jesus' own spittle is ointment for the blind. He tells of parents giving food to their children and sees himself as a mother hen gathering her chicks to herself. 'Give us this day our daily bread' is the prayer he teaches and he refuses to send the crowds away before they are fed. Indeed, feeding and nurturing are part of Jesus' whole ministry, taking the security and hospitality of the Jewish home to those who were excluded from society. For he inherited a religious tradition in which food also celebrated the healing story of Israel's relationship with God. This is brought alive today in Jewish kitchens where 'Passover is the bread of poverty, with tears and salt water, and the horseradish of bitterness. Ruth is cream and cheesecake, and the New Year is the sweetness of apples and honey. Esther comes with poppy seed, and the Maccabees with nuts.'[4]

In Jesus' hands the material becomes a sign of God's prodigality, whether at a village wedding or the feeding of the five thousand. The generosity of his parting gift to his followers, the gift of his own flesh and blood in bread and wine at the Last Supper, realized in the cross and resurrection, shows the material not subdued but transfigured with love. The soldier who pierces his side to ensure death displays instead the life-giving sacramental signs of blood and water. The presence of the risen Christ is confirmed to the disciples by the invitation to 'Touch me and see' as Jesus eats with them. Whether at Emmaus, in the Upper Room or by the lakeside, it is in the sharing of a meal that Christ is recognized, quickening the appetite for the feast of the kingdom where the poor and maimed, the blind and the lame, from east and west, north and south, will come to share God's love.

Divine diversity

Jesus' attitude was fed and sustained by the theology of the psalms which he prayed day by day and their affirmation of creation brings a healthy balance to our liturgy. Faced with Jewish apocalyptic and Greek dualism in the Bible and the scandal of the incarnation, where universal salvation is rooted in a Galilean

carpenter of the first century, we find in the Psalter the praises of
the whole world, as one worshipper recalls:

> The words of the psalms were not just sounds; the words
> were images, images of the world, images of God. The
> brief verses flashed in and out of the Catholic mass like
> bright melodic intrusions into the long rhetorical portions
> of the service. They told me that rivers clapped their hands
> and trees shouted for joy, hills leapt like yearling lambs and
> heaven sang. Days told stories and messages blew through
> the night wind.[5]

Through this symphony creation sings its own God-given
praises. The Easter Vigil offers a powerful illustration. The
church is filled with the scent and colour of spring flowers, ewers
of water, the resin of incense and bees' wax waiting to be lit. Yet,
by the time the deacon comes to sing the Exsultet, calling on the
earth in shining splendour to rejoice in the risen Saviour, we have
already struggled with the elements as the wind vies with our
attempt to light the Paschal candle from the new fire. Within
each work of God there is also paradox: we hear the refreshing
sound of water being poured into the font but we shrink from
the splash as the congregation are aspersed with it. But it is still
important for us that disturbing and contrary elements of nature
(and ourselves) are incorporated into the liturgy, rather than
regarded as an intrusion. The ambiguity is expressed in Psalm
104, often used at the Easter Vigil after the first reading of the
creation story. The streams are reinvigorating but the waters of
the raging ocean fill us with awe.

R   *Send forth your spirit, O Lord,*
     and renew the face of the earth.

> Bless the Lord, my soul!
> Lord God, how great you are,
> clothed in majesty and glory,
> wrapped in light as in a robe!   R

> You founded the earth on its base,

to stand firm from age to age.
You wrapped it with the ocean like a cloak;
the waters stood higher than the mountains.   R

You make the springs gush forth in the valleys:
they flow in between the hills.
On their banks dwell the birds of heaven;
from the branches they sing their song.   R

Roman Rite

The paradox of creation is attributed to the Wisdom of God
(*hochmah*) who in Hebrew assumes a feminine persona like God's
regenerating breath or Spirit (*ruah*), another word which takes us
beyond its grammatical gender into the feminine heart of God.
Indeed, the Psalmist explicitly depicts the divine Mother giving
birth to her whole world:

Lord, you have been our home
    from generation to generation.
Before the mountains were born,
        or you had gone into labour to bring forth the
            earth . . .

Psalm 90

At the Easter Vigil the blessing of the waters powerfully enacts
this maternal symbolism as the womb of the font immerses the
Paschal candle in the waters. A Maronite baptismal prayer reveals
the particular role of the Spirit in mothering:

As the Holy Spirit hovered over the waters at the establish-
ment of creation, so may your Holy Spirit, O Lord, hover
over this baptismal water which is a spiritual womb . . .[6]

In that wisdom God has made a world of interdependence
which Psalm 104 celebrates with delight. The stork builds her
nest on the treetops, the goats find a home in the mountains and
the rabbits hide among the rocks. At the same time, the threat
which creatures present to each other is put within boundaries:
the beasts of the forest creep out in the dark and the young lions
roar for their prey, but at dawn they steal away and the human

animal takes the stage. Judaism, which sings this psalm at New
Moon, points to God's wisdom dividing the twenty-four hours
between humankind and other animal life. The Psalmist depicts
God setting limits for earth and sea, day and night, summer and
winter (Pss. 74.13–17; 104.5–9; 148.1–6), and Robert Murray
sees in these boundaries or rules a cosmic covenant by which
God pledges security and stability for all creation while expecting
human beings as stewards of the world to maintain peace in the
cosmos by balancing and respecting the needs of its creatures and
keeping the fabric of society together with rules of justice
and righteousness. From such mutual promises, like a marriage,
flows harmony for the earth:

> On that day I will make a covenant for them,
>   with the animals of the wild,
>   with the birds of the sky and what creeps on the
>   ground.
> I will break bow, sword and war on earth,
>   and I will let them rest in safety.
>
> *Hosea 2.18*[7]

Psalm 104 reflects this mutual relationship between God's
creatures as also between God and ourselves. Plants are provided
by God for human beings to cultivate and process into bread
and wine, 'which earth has given and human hands have made',
as the offertory prayers at Mass say, showing the mystery of
our interdependence and cooperation with creation and Creator.
As yet, however, the language, never mind the practice of
cosmic covenant, has made little impact on liturgy.

The realm God gives each creature is not without its pain.
While we hear the promise that God gives to all their food in due
season, we are reminded that 'hidden in those lines there is the
objectionable mystery of the predator and the prey; there is
the dread, there is a whole world of living things seeking what
refuge there insufficiently is, there is the terrified scuttle in the
forest.'[8] For D. H. Lawrence, however, this world of God's
making necessarily involves danger and death. In his poem
'Lord's Prayer', he sees that all creatures have been given their

natural realm of power, but the nocturnal kingdom and glory of the fox spells death to the goose.

The stark reality faces worshippers at some medieval churches in south India where the external walls depict Adam and Eve with bright fruit and wily snake surrounded by fighting peacocks, a man trampled by an elephant and another spearing a lion, as well as crocodiles and whales chasing their prey.[9]

The dissonance of our present dispensation is clearly perceived by the prophets, for in their Messianic paradise the cow and the bear will graze together, the lion and the ox will eat straw, and the child and the adder will be safe together in a world where there will be no hurt or destruction (Isa. 11.6–9; 65.25; Hos. 2.18). Meanwhile, the wisdom of God remains strange and for some even offensive, but it is a wisdom whose ecological balance we disrupt at our peril, and which may ensure the variety of all kinds of species, rather than just those which suit our convenience or appeal to our feelings.

The eucharistic symphony

Behind our attitudes there often lies the arrogant assumption that ours is the only praise God wants to hear. The Welsh tell the story of how Beuno silenced the raucous frogs who dared to interrupt his serene recitation of the office, only to be challenged by the very words of the Benedicite canticle which he was chanting. Scripture itself indicts us. In the Celtic world, animals, birds and fish all sing of God's glory to human beings. Their voices are acknowledged in richly illuminated manuscripts such as the Lindisfarne Gospels, where a bounding cat and a flock of sea birds herald the good news according to Luke. And for the poet Dafydd ap Gwilym, no human voice is needed at all for worship; the thrush can be the celebrant singing a woodland mass, cloaked with a chasuble of the greenery around him, and the nightingale can be the acolyte sounding the Sanctus bell.[10] After all, the Temple was a home for the sparrow and swallow who inspired the Psalmist's praises (Ps. 84.3).

We may include the voices of all God's creatures in our praises but, according to the divine purpose, they have been co-workers, through their behaviour and natural instincts, in bringing salvation as well as in celebrating it. Camels kneeling by the well bring Isaac and Rebekah together for the future of Israel, Balaam's donkey saves his life, ravens provide food for Elijah in the desert, the lions respect Daniel's holiness and medicine from a fish saves Tobit's sight. A Syrian hymn for the morning takes us back to the archetypal story of humanity, floundering against the tide of the elements and depending on the instincts of other creatures, a prelude to God establishing a covenant with all creation.

> At the time of morning the dove was sent
> from the side of Noah the Just because of the waters of the
>   flood.
> And the dove returned to the ark bearing a branch of
>   olive,
> the sign of reconciliation and peace.

The faithfulness of the covenant continues to be fulfilled with David.

> At the time of morning, King David
> sang to his harp songs of the Holy Spirit.
> And all the animals came and assembled
> at the sweet sound of his song, as he sang halleluia.[11]

Messianic hopes are brought to fruition in the new covenant when the Son of David is carried into Jerusalem as prince of peace on a donkey. But it is perhaps the implicit cooperation of animals in the nativity story which has most captured Christian imagination and found its way into worship, drawing on the prophecy: 'The ox knows its owner and the donkey its master's crib' (Isa 1.3).

> *In praesepe positum*
>   *Sub foeno asinorum*
> *Cognoverunt Dominum*
>   *Christum, Regem coelorum.*

Laid within a manger
  Under asses' hay,
They recognized the Lord,
  Christ, the King of heaven.

> Puer nobis nascitur (*Moosburg Gradual, 1360*)

As early as the fourth century we find stone reliefs of the animals admiring the Christ child, as indeed from the same period come sculptures of Christ, Son of David, portrayed like Orpheus with harp or pipes drawing the animals to himself.[12] The image of ox and ass adoring the Word made flesh in their manger was also a powerful symbol of the faithful coming to feed from Christ in the Eucharist.

> *O magnum mysterium et admirabile sacramentum,*
> *ut animalia viderent Dominum natum iacentem in praesepio.*
> O how great the mystery, how wonderful the
>   sacrament,
> that beasts should see the newborn Lord lying in their
>   manger.

> *Christmas Matins Antiphon*

The moment in worship where we would expect to hear these praises of creation is the great Prayer of Thanksgiving at the Eucharist, yet over the centuries these diverse voices have been stifled. Earlier liturgies developed the Jewish thanksgiving of God 'who made heaven and earth, the sea and all that is in them' (Ps. 146.6; *cf.* Neh. 9.6; Acts 4.24). By the fifth century the Egyptian Liturgy of St Mark had added rivers, lakes, humankind and the pleasures of paradise. The Liturgy of St James follows the Psalmist in letting creation offer its own thanksgiving:

> It is right . . . to give thanks to you, Maker of all creation, seen and unseen . . . whom the heaven of heavens, and all their powers, the sun and moon, and all the choir of stars, earth, sea, and all that is in them, praise in song . . .

> (cf. *Psalm 148*)

But the most amazing tapestry of praise is found in a

fourth-century Syrian eucharistic prayer which turns to Psalm
104 for its inspiration.

> You set out the heavens like a vault,
> and stretch it out like a tent . . .
> you brought darkness as refreshment
> for the living creatures that move upon the earth . . .
> you divided the great sea from the land . . .
> you filled it with living creatures, small and great,
> you filled your world and adorned it
> with fragrant and healing herbs,
> with many varied living things for food and work . . .

Across the ages and continents we hear the same words in a
Springtime Eucharist from California and they can hardly be
dismissed as some trendy earth-centred liturgy when they are
actually recovering buried treasure:

> Then there is the sea, with its vast expanses
> teeming with countless creatures, creatures both small
>   and great . . .
> They all depend on you to feed them when they need it.
> You provide the food they gather,
> your open hand gives them their fill.[13]

This psalm is also sung at Pentecost when we give thanks for
the gift of many tongues and its polychromatic chorus of praise
has much to teach us about how to enjoy and value the pluralism
of the world. The Corrymeela community, which has so courageously brought Irish people together across the Protestant/
Catholic divide, composed a liturgy called a Celebration of
Diversity with these words as the centrepiece. The beauty of God
in rivers and hills, goats and badgers, all seems uncontroversial
enough but the message of diversity as a divine ordinance rather
than an accident of nature has implications which we cannot
escape, especially as we hear the psalm read by two alternating
voices, concluding:

> Lord, you have made so *many* things,
> How wisely you have made them all!

The earth is filled with your creatures.
All *O Lord, our Lord how great you are.*

Psalm 104.24, 1

Pluralism is God's will and God's glory.

Here are theological and ecological grounds for psalmody in liturgy to leaven the often narrow world of Christian scripture. Especially on occasions where Mass is only possible if a deacon or lay minister administers communion from the reserved sacrament, psalms such as 34, 104, 145 or 147 at the opening of worship or before communion could enrich a rite without a eucharistic prayer and offer a broader horizon of the kingdom.

Taste and see

It is in the Eucharist that this realm of God's making, so different from our own warped prejudices, is shown to us. Here we see God's best intentions for creation and the wonder is that God chooses to reveal this mystery of grace through the most ordinary bodily sense of taste. Conversation and dialogue engage us; taste makes us share the same food and inwardly transforms us. We find this expressed in a communion anthem from Psalm 34, which invites the faithful to relish the sweetness and goodness of the Lord. It appears in the baptismal homily of 1 Peter (2.3) and at the Easter Baptism and Eucharist in Jerusalem in the fourth century, but its use spread to the Lenten Liturgy of the Pre-sanctified Gifts in Syria and beyond to Armenia, Spain and Ireland. Anglican and Reformed Churches have restored it to the Eucharist.

Taste and see how sweet the Lord is: alleluia!
I will always bless the Lord,
    whose praise is ever in my mouth: alleluia!
The Lord redeems the life of God's servants and will not
    abandon those who hope in God: alleluia!
Glory to the Father, and to the Son, and to the Holy
    Spirit,
    for ever and ever: alleluia, Amen.[14]

The title of this psalm describes its setting as the time when David feigned madness to escape his enemy (1 Sam. 21.13–14), or as the Hebrew puts it, 'when he disguised his taste'. Taste was synonymous with good sense and a balanced frame of mind. And the food of the Eucharist is the stuff of life through which God redeems us from past sin and makes us a people to bear hope for the world, keeping us sane in body and mind in every circumstance.

To taste also means to discover our individual identity. The Brazilian psychoanalyst and philosopher Rubem Alves maintains that the Latin languages preserve an intuition in their derivation of 'knowledge' and 'taste' from the same root (*sapere*). The emotionally damaged development and lack of self-esteem that are at the centre of eating disorders, abusing both food and self, offer tragic corroboration. Where tasting is a real experience, it changes both the raw material and ourselves:

> Cooking is a liturgical ritual. In it eternal truth, our eternal search for happiness is reenacted: the 'pleasure principle' takes the 'reality principle' in its hands, burns it on an altar, and its 'soothing odour' and good taste make love with our body. Not dualism but dialectics. They are brought together, 'without confusion', and a new reality comes into being. [15]

In the Eucharist, moreover, eating is not a guilty secret as with Adam and Eve, the angst-ridden diet of the obsessive, the solitary meal of the lonely, or an expensive dinner party to which only influential people are invited. The Eucharist is the sharing of Christ's love and friendship together, a meal where guests value and cherish each other. Alves continues:

> Now the guests are transformed . . . They eat together, they become 'companions' . . . The meaning of the word is very suggestive. It comes from the Latin '*com*' (with) and '*panis*' (bread) . . . the purpose of a dinner party is not the pragmatical end of nourishment and not only the pleasures of eating. It is hoped that eating together will become an

occasion of companionship, friendship. The guests assimilate the food. The ritual assimilates the guests.[16]

Archimandrite Vasileios, an abbot from Mount Athos, points to the paradoxical inclusiveness of the Eucharist which forms a pattern for our lives. Distances are made to disappear as the priest prays for all who journey by sea or land or are in distress as if they were there in church with us. The mystery of the liturgy brings together in one place those who in worldly terms are scattered. Yet we are not crowded together with some mono-chrome programme of church life or identical opinions. 'The love of the Trinity expands space into paradise; a paradise of freedom, released from care, fear and hatred. There is no opacity: everything shines like crystal. There is no lack of space caused by impenetrability; everyone has ample room: "What you commanded has been done, and still there is room" (Luke 14.22).'[17] But it is only by taking thought for the worldwide and the universal as we are drawn into Christ through our worship that we can order our own affairs bounded by time and space. We cannot find salvation apart from the peace of the whole world. This cosmic and eschatological vision has yet to influence much of Western liturgy but it is there in the hymns of the Wesleys and the rarely used Litany of the *Book of Common Prayer*, and we are beginning to tap the sources of other traditions. Like the all-embracing colours of a Syrian altar with its fiery red for the universe, the verdant green of earth and the white of holy Church, worship and worshippers need to be both diverse and united.

> The outcasts of Israel God gathers together,
> It is God who is healing the brokenhearted
> and binding up their wounds . . .
> who makes peace to be your borders
> and satisfies you with the finest wheat.
>
> *Psalm 147.2–3, 14*

For some people, including other traditions is a threat and including others who are not like us arouses even more anxiety. The two often go together. We may not be talking about refugees from other races and cultures but just incomers who have moved into an old English village. The model of worship, however, is that 'each new arrival does not make for discomfort, which provokes mistrust, but for an increased breadth, the provision of new space and joy'.[18]

After all, the noble David of Psalm 34, who bids us taste and see how good the Lord is, writes these words from the experience of being a refugee from his own family, seeking help among his nation's enemies and then pretending to be an imbecile to escape danger. His whole outlook is that of the '*anawim*, 'the socially marginal, who no longer expect the dominant society to succour them, and so they look to Yahweh as the alternative source of help'.[19] It is the thanksgiving of the powerless whose helplessness has enabled them to see God's vision for the world where evil is doomed and the brokenhearted are saved.

> In the Lord my soul shall find her praise:
>   let the humble ('*anawim*) hear and be glad.
> Tell out the greatness of the Lord with me:
>   and let us raise God's name up high together . . .
> This poor soul cried out and the Lord heard me,
>   and saved me from all my troubles . . .
> Young lions may suffer want and hunger,
>   but those who seek the Lord lack no good thing.
>   *Psalm 34.2–3, 6, 10*

A foretaste of the kingdom

Our communion, that 'foretaste of the heavenly banquet prepared for all', as Methodists call it, changes our lifestyle. The Christ we receive calls us to live a transfigured life. 'We have seen the true Light', Orthodox sing after communion. We return to embody the vision of the world we see in Christ. Coventry Cathedral incorporates this truth into stained glass windows whose refracted light communicants can only see on their way back from the altar. Our whole vocation and mission flow from the feast we share, a feast which should overturn our values and prejudices and change our view of the company we keep and of invited but absent guests.

The psalms, like a river, carry this experience from the altar into our daily life. From the Eucharist they take the richness of the source and feed it into the praise of the Daily Office, as we sing the same words again, enriched with their sacramental meaning. From there they flow into thanksgiving for our meals, prayers by the bedside of the sick or hasty reminders of God when we are in trouble. By these words the most ordinary and uninspiring parts of our life are hallowed. Christian tradition has repeatedly affirmed this unity of work and worship and, when liturgy has been silent on the theme, the medieval sculptors reminded the Church that the farmer feeding sprouts to his goats belongs beside the Lord sending the disciples out to disciple the world.[20]

Our communion with God through the material takes us back to the root goodness which God gave creation. Day by day we feed on God's goodness and the tasting creates an emotional bond of love and security in which we mature.

> The eyes of all look up to you
> nor for an instant doubt.
> Again upon the dry and parched
> send down your sweetest dew.
> For wherever you water it,
> the root of good will sprout.
> *Eighth Century Chinese Gloria* cf. *Psalm 145.14–15*[21]

When we taste this fullness of God's providence, we taste the presence of God, for creation cannot exist apart from the Creator. Philip Sherrard concludes from this biblical insight that 'creatures not only take their being from God but are kept in being by remaining in God . . . creation is nothing less than the manifestation of God's hidden Being: the other world is this world, this is the other world. If the kingdom of God can come on earth, it is because in essence the earth is the kingdom of God.'[22] Bread and wine have been changed from wheat and grapes but they have in them some original God-given essence that does not need any radical alteration to convey the divine.

Their natural being already reveals the nature of God. The message to all who ravish the world's natural resources is clear: destroy the earth and you lose sight of God.

And what is revealed is both the original goodness in which creation was conceived and the goodness to which God draws us in the kingdom to come. The taste of Eden quickens an appetite for paradise. This hope is expressed by Jews as they prepare for prayer by putting on the tallith, or prayer-shawl, with words which recall Psalm 104:

> Just as I cover myself with a robe (*tallith*) in this world, so may my soul deserve to be robed in a beautiful robe in the world to come, in the garden of Eden.

The same psalm has been sung at Vespers in the Church since about the year 500. Its meditation on the boundaries of light and dark makes us reflect on the mysterious providence of the changing hours. But in the Orthodox service, the way that the singing combines with the liturgical action has led some writers to interpret this as a hymn describing the beginning of creation. The royal doors into the sanctuary symbolize the gates of paradise; the incense wafting through the church represents the Spirit, the breath of God upon the waters of creation. The closed doors make us feel like Adam and Eve shut out of Eden and their opening, accompanied by light, heralds the coming of Christ to open the kingdom for us.[23]

> You water the mountains from your dwelling on high;
> with the fruit of your works the earth shall be satisfied.
> You grow grass for the cattle and corn for human needs,
> to bring forth bread from the earth,
> and wine gladdens the human heart . . .
> All creatures look up to you
> to give them their food in good time.
> As you give it to them, they gather it;
> as you open your hand,
> all creation is filled with kindness . . .
> You send forth your Spirit and they are created
> and you renew the face of the earth.

May the glory of the Lord endure for ever:
may the Lord rejoice in his works . . .

Psalm 104.14–15, 27–31

It is the sharing of that food together that opens our eyes to the true glory of God's realm. The great Danish Lutheran preacher and hymn-writer, Nicolai Grundtvig, was very fond of this psalm, especially its reference to 'wine which gladdens the human heart'. He points out that, though religious and secular lifestyles have common ground in the material world, they differ radically. Drinking songs may say the same thing as the Psalmist but that does not mean that psalms are drinking songs nor do drinking songs become psalms. For people of faith value wine as a gift of grace which God has given not just to quench thirst but to draw us into communion with each other and with God. When we taste with faith, we see before us the kingdom whose guests are chosen by God, not us, whose God-given differences are to be relished and cherished, whose gifts are to be nurtured and shared, and we find that we are filled with the joy of God.

Only there, in the Church's gathering
Does daily bread become eternal.
Only there does the wine's fruit
Have the taste of heaven as the power of God,
And create with blessing the joy of the heart.[24]

TEN

A New Song for the Earth

A living sacrifice

> For all that is in the heavens and on the earth
> is yours, Lord . . .
> for from you all things come
> and from your own hand we have given back to you.

David's prayer, dedicating gifts for building the Temple (1 Chron. 29 *cf.* Pss. 24.1; 50.12; 89.11), reveals the paradox of our relationship of grace with God. All power is in God's hands and all that we have comes from God, but, if we are to celebrate God's generosity in a communal way and visibly hallow the goodness of the material creation, we must offer back in thanksgiving what God has first given us. Even the prophets who angrily challenge people who try to buy off God with habitual gifts lacking in generosity or justice allow that some offerings may be acceptable.

> Not for your sacrifices can I fault you;
> your burnt-offerings are before me continually . . .
> If I were hungry, I would not tell you,
> for the world and all its fullness is mine . . .
> Offer to God the sacrifice of thanksgiving
> and pay your vows to the Most High.
>
> *Psalm 50.8, 12, 14*

Here it is the daily sacrifice (*'olah*) that the prophet rejects, for it has become a debased currency to pay off God. This 'ascent offering' was completely burnt on the altar as a pleasing odour to the Lord and therefore might be falsely regarded as something of a bribe for God's goodwill. The thank-offering (*todah*) was only partly burnt, the remainder being shared between worshippers, priests and family, in a common meal. The fact that worshippers partook of the food indicated the special grace which God had shown them and which had brought them to offer this particular sacrifice.

God seeks our offering so that we may learn to see how our lives have been shaped by divine grace. Thanksgiving changes our appreciation of the past, the way we continue to value life, received from God's hand, and indeed our whole perspective on what is important.

> Those who bring thanksgiving as their sacrifice honour
> me.
> To those who go the right way
> I will show the salvation of God.
>
> *Psalm 50.23 (Offertory, A Prayer Book for Australia)*

Offering becomes an exchange of lives as well as gifts. The giving and receiving are all part of the bonding relationship through which we grow closer to God. God has given us this commandment and the resources to fulfil it not so that we may execute a duty and be done with it but to nurture us in an ever more fulfilled life. The more we enter into the mystery of who we are and what gifts lie waiting within us to be discovered, the more we are drawn to the person of the God who made us and gave us this means of grace to find and be found. The prayers of the Methodist Covenant Service open us up to the full realization of what that divine purpose might be.

> Let me be employed for you or laid aside for you . . .
> let me be full, let me be empty;
> let me have all things, let me have nothing . . .
> I freely and wholeheartedly yield all things
> to your pleasure and disposal.
> And now, glorious and blessed God,

Father, Son, and Holy Spirit,
you are mine and I am yours.

From John Wesley's own directions we know that the inspiration for these last words which characterize the whole service came from the Psalmist:

I am thine, O save me:
for I have sought thy commandments.

Psalm 119.94 (BCP)[1]

In contrast to the wicked who only pursue their own arrogance and greed, the believer has searched out in mind and heart what God's will really is: the quest to be what God wants has made them God's own servant, loving and beloved of God. In such a relationship the emptiness, the struggle, the uselessness of our lives can become an offering to God and not only in word, for the Covenant Service proceeds, after the Lord's Prayer, to the Offertory and the Eucharist where we hold out our hands, heart and mouth to hold our incarnate Lord.

Thus the most precious gift we have to offer, our real 'liturgy' as Paul put it (Rom. 12.1), is ourselves, body and soul, 'a living sacrifice'. This view of sacrifice had already been powerfully advocated in Judaism during the Exile. Ezekiel, for example, foresees the day when God will accept the choicest of the people's gifts at a rebuilt Temple but the real 'pleasing odour' of sacrifice will be the offering of the people themselves (Ezek. 20.40–1).

The offering of worship, therefore, reveals something unique about ourselves. 'It is the sacrament of yourselves that is set upon the Lord's Table; the sacrament of yourselves that you receive. To what you are you will be responding "Amen", and you will be agreeing to your response.'[2] At the same time, the gifts and person we offer show the kind of God who created us to be what we are. As a foretaste of the kingdom, the Eucharist also holds within its mystery the promise of what God may yet make of us. The first-fruits of wheat and vine are symbols of our potential growth.

Christ gave instruction to his disciples to offer to God the first-fruits from God's own creation, not as if to one who is in need of them, but so that they might not be unfruitful or ungrateful . . . This oblation the Church has received from the apostles and offers throughout the whole world to the God who gives us as our food the first-fruits of God's own gifts in the new covenant . . .[3]

Love exchanged

Our offering cannot be made in isolation from the community of faith. There is a popular view that we may worship God in our back garden, though fewer do, we may think, than those who say they can – and this is small comfort to those without gardens. The God whose nature is to share seeks a people forged out of diverse gifts and characters to be the ikon of divine grace. The Hebrew word for offering (*qarav*) has the sense of causing to come near. The bringing of a gift draws us nearer to God and, when shared in a sacrificial meal, nearer to one another.

Remarkably, in the Christian Eucharist there is little about sharing at the offertory itself. A notable exception is the much neglected set of offertory sentences in the *Book of Common Prayer.*

Blessed be the man that provideth for the sick and needy:
the Lord shall deliver him in the time of trouble.

Psalm 41.1

Most explicit is the Zairean Mass (1988) where the gifts are offered at the altar with the entire congregation proclaiming:

O priest of God, here are our gifts. Receive them.
They show our spirit of solidarity and sharing
and that we love one another
as the Lord has loved us.[4]

Again, the Passover tradition with its communal hospitality has lessons for Christians. Just as the thank-offering of the Temple was shared with other worshippers, Passover lambs were also frequently shared, particularly among poorer people, and hospitality to guests is still an important part of the festival. Hosts provide gifts for others to offer and share as well as giving

on their own account. Maundy Thursday demonstrates a strong
sense of belonging together, enacted both in the foot-washing
and the communion. It is the offering of a community, drawing
upon the same psalm as Passover.

> How can I repay the Lord
> for his goodness to me?
> The cup of salvation I will raise;
> I will call on the Lord's name.
>
> . . .
>
> Your servant, Lord, your servant am I;
> you have loosened my bonds.
>
> A thanksgiving sacrifice I make:
> I will call on the Lord's name.
> My vows to the Lord I will fulfil
> before all the people.
>
> *Psalm 116 (Roman Rite)*

At every Eucharist the gifts which are prepared by some, carried
by others and shared by all indicate that the liturgy expresses an
exchange of offering and love among the people of God. The
sacrament can never separate the physical and spiritual needs of
people nor become a private communion with God.

Charles Williams saw that this principle of 'exchanges of
love', bearing burdens for each other, living for others, could
transform the whole of society; for we are 'caught by others and
lifted into an exchange of grace – into others by others, into
Another by Another'.[5] He found an obvious paradigm for this
relationship of grace in marriage, a physical and spiritual union
of trust where husband and wife mutually agree, the one to
abandon his seed to the other, the other to receive in herself
another's seed. The rings and crowns in the marriage service may
be powerful signs, but the real matter of the sacrament is the
union of two people, body and soul. Perhaps the Anglo-Norman
Church used the Mass of the Holy Trinity to make marriages
more festive but it reflects well the divine pattern of mutual
giving and receiving. It is a pity that psalmody at weddings has
become rare, because it springs from a corporate understanding

of relationships which broadens our introspective view into a joy to be shared with all the community.

> Trust in the Lord and do good:
> and you shall dwell in the land and feed in safe pastures.
> Let the Lord be your delight:
> and he will grant you your heart's desire.
>
> Psalm 37.3–4 (*Marriage*, A Prayer Book for Australia)

Charles Williams drew from marriage a parallel with our relationship with God, especially in the communion of the Eucharist, where, 'to effect the mystery of unity, we ourselves receive of that which is his what he himself received of that which is ours'.[6]

The world's high priest

> What is a child of earth that you should care for us?
> Yet you have made us lack little of God,
> with glory and honour you have crowned us.
>
> Psalm 8.4–5

Our offering does not just involve the human community. We are called not to neglect or exploit creation as an expendable asset and boast of our own achievements, but fulfil the privilege of the spiritual, intellectual and emotional faculties God has given us and become, as George Herbert said, 'the world's high priest'.[7] We are not tourists of nature but fellow worshippers. 'We are the word by which the world expresses itself, by which it speaks to God: it depends on us whether it blasphemes or it prays.'[8]

The artist David Jones argued that this is the gift of every human being, whether they are particularly religious or not.

> A man can not only smell roses (some beasts may do that . . .) but he can and does and ought to pluck roses and he can predicate of roses such and such. He can make a *signum* of roses. He can make attar of roses. He can garland them and make anathemata of them. Which is, presumably, the *kind* of thing he is meant to do. Anyway, there's no one

else to do it. Angels can't nor can the beasts. No wonder then that Theology regards the body as a unique good. Without body: without sacrament. Angels only: no sacrament. Beasts only: no sacrament. Man: sacrament at every turn and all levels of the 'profane' and 'sacred', in the trivial and in the profound, no escape from sacrament.[9]

Our ability to make a transcendent symbol of something material can be seen in the food of Passover, the kindling of the Sabbath light, the water and oil of baptism or the offering of bread and wine at the Eucharist. The Eastern and Celtic traditions of Christianity, have, like Judaism, always taken that sacramental spirituality into every part of everyday life. As the Jewish home has its Mezuzah scroll on the doorpost, each Orthodox home has its shrine in a corner with ikon and lamp; and the whole landscape of Eastern Europe and the Celtic West is marked with holy places, wells and stones. These shrines are not for decoration or superstition; they are places of prayer where heaven and earth touch each other. The Armenian *khatchkar*, a stone slab carved with a cross, is an example of a symbol through which people seek protection and healing. At its consecration, the cross is washed with water and wine, anointed and named and the psalm suggests both the priestly blessing of Israel (Num. 6.26) and a sign of blessing such as a banner or standard in the Temple.

> Alleluia! The light of your face, O Lord,
> has been signed upon us.
>
> *Psalm 4.6*[10]

This priesthood of the material world should be shown in the Eucharistic Prayer, the Anaphora, as Eastern Christians call it, the 'lifting up' of ourselves and all creation to God in Christ. Whatever the origin of the opening dialogue 'Lift up your hearts', its roots lie deep in Hebrew prayer. Lifting up (*nasa'*) describes the action of hands and eyes in prayer, particularly at the offering of a sacrifice.

> Therefore I have gazed upon you in the sanctuary
> to see your power and glory . . .
> Therefore I will bless you all my life,

in your name I will lift up my hands.
As with the rich food of sacrifice my soul shall be satisfied.

Psalm 63.2–5

The Hebrew word also carries the sense of atoning for sin, whether it be Aaron's vestments, the ritual of the scapegoat or Ezekiel's prophetic and priestly action (Exod. 28.38; Lev. 16.22; Ezek. 4.4). Jesus' own ministry was marked by the lifting up of the eyes in prayer before sacramental acts of healing and breaking bread, and the first Christian apostles use the same language of the sacrifice of Christ (Mark 9.2; John 6.5; Heb. 7.27; 1 Pet. 2.24). For the medieval German mystic Heinrich Seuse, singing the words of the Sursum Corda at Mass brought the priestly privilege of offering the whole world to God: 'I gather round me all the creatures which God ever created in heaven, on earth, and in all the elements, each one severally with its name, whether birds of the air, beasts of the forest, fishes of the water, leaves and grass of the earth, or the innumerable sand of the sea.'[11] In modern Western rites the offering of creation is largely ignored: two eucharistic prefaces do celebrate the wonder and providence of nature, both resonant with the Psalmist's praise.

All things are of your making,
all times and seasons obey your laws,
but you have chosen to create us in your own image,
setting us over the whole world in all its wonder,
You have made us stewards of your creation,
to praise you day by day for the marvels of your wisdom
    and power.

cf. *Psalms 8.6; 96.2–3*

From the beginning you have created all things
and all your works echo the silent music of your praise,
In the fullness of time you made us in your image,
the crown of all creation.

cf. *Psalms 19.3–4; 8.5*[12]

The Eucharist seems to imply that we cannot give thanks to God without offering the world of creation. Deprived of altar, bread and wine, on the steppes of Asia, Teilhard de Chardin still brings to God an offering of the material.

> I, your priest, will offer you the work and suffering of the world on the altar of the whole earth. Over there the sun comes to shed light on the extreme edge of the eastern sky of the day . . . My paten and my chalice are the depths of a soul wide open to all the forces which, in a moment, will rise from all points of the globe and converge upon the Spirit.[13]

The sculptor Barbara Hepworth could express in her work the tangible form and spiritual power of the luminous Night Sky, the towering spirit of the Dryad tree and the smooth yet powerful flow of the River. Her childhood inspiration was travelling with her father over the West Riding hills: here she could identify herself, like a priest, with the gift offered at her hands.

> There was the sensation of moving physically over the contours of fullnesses and concavities, through hollows and over peaks – feeling, touching, seeing, through mind and hand and eye. The sensation has never left me. I, the sculptor, *am* the landscape.[14]

The Psalmist's vision of gathering the universe before God included peoples of all races, whatever their background of faith. The new world of God's making would mean all nations coming to acknowledge their Creator with awe and offering their glory, their distinctive strengths and the inner beauty and wonder of human potential that only unfolds in worship. Such a new world demands a new song.[15]

> Sing to the Lord a new song:
> sing to the Lord, all the earth . . .
> Give to the Lord, you families of the peoples,
> give to the Lord glory and strength . . .
> bring an offering and come into the courts of the Lord.
> Worship the Lord in the beauty of holiness:
> let all the earth tremble as if to give birth
> > before the Lord.   *Psalm 96.1, 7–9*

We may remember that the Roman canon refers to the accept-able sacrifice of 'Abraham, our father in faith, and the bread and wine offered by your priest Melchisedek', who, for the mystic Abhishiktananda, recall 'those priests who continue to offer to God their daily oblations of bread and rice, of flowers, lights and incense, in the temples and sacred places of India'.[16] Like the psalm, our eucharistic thanksgiving has a wide vision.

The agricultural year, shamefully neglected by modern lec-tionaries, provides many opportunities to bring the whole creation and our part in it to God. Though sowing may take place at various times, Rogationtide focuses more keenly, even anxiously, on the expectations that lie between promise and fulfilment. Psalm 67, often used both at Rogation and Harvest, illustrates this tension, depending on whether the Hebrew describing the harvest yield is thought to be past or future. The ambiguity of time and the anticipatory prayer and praise suggest that it was sung before harvest. Judaism has traditionally recited it between Passover and the harvest celebrations of Shavuot (Pentecost),

> Let the peoples praise you, O God;
> let all the peoples praise you.
> Then shall the earth bring forth her increase,
> and God, our own God, will bless us.
> *Psalm 67.5–6 (Rogation Gradual,* Common Worship)

The promise of fruitfulness is more likely to be fulfilled because we have first entrusted our labour to God, the source of all growth, and such a sense of God alongside us in the perils of farming encourages both much needed patience and self-worth.

The 'not yet' mood of expectation awaiting fulfilment is echoed in various customs involving walking in procession either around the church, around sown fields or 'beating the bounds' of the parish. They remind us that the earth, including our earth in our locality, is the Lord's: God is not to be confined to the sanctuary. And our walking from church brings prayer and blessing to the environment. The physical act of walking also reminds us that we are on a journey both through the seasons of the year and in our own spiritual growth. We cannot stay still: we grow or we wither.

Liturgical movement concludes the agricultural year with a procession bringing the harvest produce to the altar. All the watching and waiting are fulfilled in this array of abundance and the joy of praise. There is no substitute for a church thick with the earthy smell of carrots and beetroot mixed with the sweet smell of apples. Tinned food or monetary gifts are often good practical expressions of charity but to exclude the fruits of nature is simply to remove ourselves further from the divine providence of creation.

> Praise to you, O God, in your holy place,
> *To you we bring the thanks we promised.*
> You hear our prayer, to you all human beings shall come.
> *Our sins have done too much damage,*
> *but you forgive us.*
> Happy are those you choose to come and bring you gifts:
> *We shall be filled with the goodness of your house.*
> You crown the year of your goodness:
> *The meadows are clothed with flocks,*
> *the valleys stand so thick with corn,*
> *they shout for joy and sing!*
> Psalm 65.1–4, 11, 13 (Harvest Processional)

The world which we offer includes those who have died. The tragedy of bereavement today is that remembrance of the dead is confined to an artificial congregation of people who do not normally celebrate the faith together. The death of a loved one may cause a person's whole world to collapse because they belong to no other community outside the family. The Kaddish, the Jewish prayer of mourners, does not even mention the departed but prays for the coming kingdom. Even death cannot detach them from the whole community that awaits God's realm of love and truth. Jewish mystics envisaged the gates of paradise being opened for the dead in response to the power of the congregation's response to the Kaddish. The prayer may have been inspired by Psalm 145, of which it was said that 'whoever recites this psalm daily is assured of their part in the world to come'.[17]

> One generation shall praise your works to another,
> *And proclaim your mighty acts.*
> All your creation shall give you thanks,
> *And your faithful servants shall bless you.*
> They shall tell of the glory of your kingdom
> and speak of your great power.
> *My mouth shall speak the praise of the Lord.*
> *And let all flesh bless God's holy name for ever and ever.*
>> *Psalm 145.4, 10–11, 21 (Responsory for the Departed)*

The opening of the Roman Requiem Mass places us in a community on a common pilgrimage, sharing our needs with all flesh, but this psalm only tends to be used when the text is sung in Latin.

> *Give them eternal rest, O Lord,*
> *and may your light shine on them for ever.*
>> To you praise is due, O God, in Zion,
>> and to you shall the vow be paid in Jerusalem.
>> You hear our prayer and to you all flesh shall come
>> because of their sins.
>> Though our sins have overwhelmed us,
>> you will forgive them.
>>> *Psalm 65*

Gregory the Great saw in these words a vision of the Church gathering its harvest in a net embracing every kind of fish, rich and poor, strong and weak. 'Thus, we hear the psalmist say, "All flesh will come to you". This net will be universally filled when it encompasses the sum of the human race at its end.'[18]

Redeeming the world

In worship not only is the whole creation offered to God in thanksgiving: the world witnesses the redeeming love of God and shares in the joy of liberation. If all things are created by God, then they bear the imprint of the divine grace and purpose.

The theologian Richard Hooker concluded that 'all things are therefore partakers of God, whose offspring they are; God's influence is in them'.[19] Looking to the peace and justice that God's Anointed will bring, the Psalmist describes the offering of creation in the language of priestly sacrifice.

O God, give the King your judgments:
R   *And your righteousness to the son of a king.*
May the mountains lift up [from *nasa'*] their offering of
        peace:
R   *And the hills prosper the people with righteousness.*
May he defend the right of the poor amongst the people:
R   *Save the children of the needy and crush the oppressor.*
May there be an abundance of grain on the earth:
R   *Even high upon the hills let it grow strong and bear fruit.*
                    Psalms 72.1–4, 16 (Passiontide Responsory)

On Good Friday, following a tradition from earliest Christianity, the cross is placed before the congregation to be venerated, and all join in a chant of praise for the salvation of the world revealed in Christ. The Roman Rite only uses the first verse of Psalm 67 and this is also the Orthodox practice, where the priest recites the verse at the close of each part of the Royal Hours, ascribed to the fourth-century Cyril of Alexandria. Psalms were often abbreviated in liturgy to a single verse and probably the whole psalm was originally sung around the cross. Anglicans have developed the rite in this way, helping us see this moment of personal and congregational adoration as the dawning of a universal hope. The final promise of the Psalmist declares that God's liberating power not only draws the nations to share this salvation with praise and joy but causes the earth to yield a new harvest of fruitfulness. Inspired by the priestly blessing of Aaron, the psalm becomes on Good Friday a celebration of Christ's priesthood for the world.

Antiphon: We worship your cross, O Lord,
        and we praise and glorify your holy resurrection;
        for by the wood of the cross
        joy has come to the whole world.

God be gracious to us and bless us:
R   *And make the light of your face to shine upon us.*
That your way may be known on earth,
your power to save among all nations.
R   *Let the peoples praise you, O God;*
         let all the peoples praise you.
Then shall the earth yield her harvest,
and God, our God, will bless us.
The antiphon is repeated.

The universal blessing of the passion is demonstrated in the
Syrian liturgy in a dramatic rite both on Good Friday and Easter
Day, as well as other occasions in the year. Prayers are said for
the abundance of fruits and their protection from blight and
sultry winds. The priest then holds high a large cross and blesses
the four corners of the world. The liturgy draws upon ancient
traditions of Jerusalem as the navel of the earth and the burial
place of Adam, where the four directions separated to enclose his
body and returned to entomb it. On Golgotha, the Cross became
the Tree of Life uniting the four directions of the world, and the
blood and water from Christ's side washed Adam, brought him
to life and returned him to paradise.[20]

On some of the earliest Christian stone reliefs we find creation
gathered around the cross depicted as the Tree of Life with
animals and birds feeding from its branches. The Anglo-Saxon
Bewcastle Cross depicts a tree encompassing in a harmonious
chain various birds and beasts. The fruitfulness of this eschatological garden, planted by Christ's passion, is vividly carved in
the Syrian seventh- and eighth-century stone crosses of Kerala
and China, where the four rivers of Eden flow and lotus flowers
blossom from the root of the cross.[21] The Psalmist knew that
God's intended inheritance for us is like a fruitful vineyard; a
community watered by a river whose streams make glad the city
of God, where the enmity between nations is ended for ever (Ps.
80, 46). Such images Jesus himself took from the Scriptures, not
least the psalms (John 15 *cf*. Ps. 80; Matt. 13.31–2 *cf*. Ps.
104.16–17).

Easter proclaims the vindication of Christ and the truth that all creation shares in the fruits of redemption. This may be depicted in churches decked with lilies and an Easter Garden but Rogation, falling within Eastertide, brings together the theological promise and the agricultural world awaiting harvest.

> Sing to the Lord a new song,
> for he has done marvellous things . . .
> His own right hand and his holy arm
> have won for him the victory . . .
> Let the sea thunder and all that fills it,
> the world and all that dwell upon it.
> Let the rivers clap their hands
> and let the hills ring out together before the Lord,
>   for he comes to judge the earth.
> *Psalm 98.1, 7–9 (Rogation Gradual,* Common Worship)

As we have seen, the Eucharist is a foretaste of this paradise, the fruit of the cross, and in this sacrament Christ opens the door to a new world, as Ephrem describes:

> The path to the Tree of Life was shut off
> by the blade of the Cherub's sword,
> but now the Lord of that Tree
> has given himself as food for all peoples.
> Whereas Eden's other trees were provided
> for Adam of old to eat,
> for us the very Planter of the Garden
> has become food for our souls.
> Whereas we had left that Garden
> along with Adam when he left it behind,
> now that the sword has been removed by the lance,
> we may return there.[22]

Oases of this rich spirituality may be found in the West. Among the Ambrosian Lenten prefaces we praise Christ 'who has opened for us, through his obedience, the way of return to paradise from which we were cast out through eating of the forbidden tree'. Charles Wesley celebrates our taste of the heavenly feast, which makes our heart dance for joy at the paradise we have already found. And the Anglo-Catholic Lionel Muirhead saw the paradise of love in the cosmic Redeemer, worshipped by rich and poor of countless lands, from whose mystic rood life-giving streams engender fruits of love.[23]

Creation joins in this adoration. The Early Church saw in a bird's opening wings a symbol of the cross. Beasts and dragons play in homage at Christ's feet on the Ruthwell Cross. With overtones of Hindu worship, elephants in an Indian church relief spray the cross with water.[24] The writers of the gospels themselves see the saving work of Christ reflected in the failing light of the sun, the cloud of darkness covering the whole land, the earthquake and splitting open of rocks. In some Eastern rites, all nature was called to acclaim God's redemption sealed at the communion itself, making the most intimate moment universal as if we were receiving Christ on behalf of all creation. A single verse remains in Orthodox and Armenian liturgies, but this East Syrian rite gives the whole symphony.

> O praise the Lord of heaven,
> *The Son who gave us his Body and Blood . . .*
> Praise him, all his host,
> *The Son who gave us his Body and Blood.*
> Praise him, sun and moon,
> *The Son who gave us his Body and Blood.*
> Praise him, all you shining stars,
> *The Son who gave us his Body and Blood.*
>
> *Psalm 148*[25]

The polyphony of life

The power of the psalms to carry this hope and joy owes much to the fact that they are songs which draw on our breath and resonate with lips and tongue. This is prayer which calls for an attentive posture of the body and a readiness to share pain and faith as we respond to others singing or sing as one body.

> I will offer in his dwelling an oblation with great gladness,
> I will sing and speak praises unto the Lord.
>
> *Psalm 27.8 (Offertory, Church in Wales)*

The physical act of singing demonstrates that worship is the offering of all life, body and soul, individual and community, humanity and all creation, with all our contrasting and conflicting experiences of love, betrayal, fear and desire.

> A psalm is calm for the soul, an arbiter of peace . . . it softens the passion of the soul and brings sense to its unruliness. A psalm brings together friendships, unites the separated, reconciles enemies . . . It makes a home in the wilderness, it brings wisdom to the market; to beginners it is a start, for those progressing it gives growth, to those who are finishing their course it is a support.[26]

Psalmody gives life a form, cherished and integrated by the grace of God. Dietrich Bonhoeffer understood that this integrity protects us from fanaticism, and that Hebrew Scripture gives Christianity a vital and wholesome balance in this respect.

> There is, however, always the danger in every strong love that one will lose with it, as one might say, the polyphony of life. I mean, God in eternity wants to be loved with the whole heart, not so that earthly love is impaired or weakened under its influence, but so that, in a way, it acts as a *cantus firmus* to which the other voices of life resound as counterpoints.[27]

The Gloria, sung at the end of the psalm in the Daily Office, roots all our experiences, good and bad, in the inclusive realm of God's grace, where alone despair and anger can be transformed into glory. The monastic practice of bowing the head at the Gloria is a physical acknowledgment of offering all life, unresolved pain along with unbelievable joy, to God.

The singing is not an end in itself. It may indeed become a weapon to exclude others, a source of idolized pride in a group of musicians when human sound drowns the voice of God. The value of the psalms is that they are not just human artistry but the word of God, God speaking through us and to us in prayer. Through them God transforms us, personally and socially, always keeping true to our human nature while drawing us into a new world of hope. Through them the reality of daily life and the reality of God become one. 'Don't wait for a miracle', the Yiddish proverb goes, 'say the Psalms.'

Though she worked in silent stone, Barbara Hepworth continually explored the power of music as she sculpted hollowed spaces and strings held in tension, suggesting, like their titles, rhythm and resonance. Her chosen epitaph for herself was *Cantate Domino* (1958), a bronze sculpture of two wings soaring upwards in birdlike transcendency, one pointing beyond the other as if to an unattained destiny. The base has a rooted network and the parted wings are linked by a flowing loop, indicating an openness to new life. The whole figure gives the impression of God at our roots and God beyond us, to whom we reach out, the God in whom earth and heaven are one. The psalms of her title sing of the God who comes to make of us a new creation and whose wonder may cause us, at any time, on any day, to proclaim

Sing to the Lord a new song!

Acknowledgments

The author would like to record his appreciation to John Eaton, whose work on the psalms has been a continual source of inspiration, and to Rabbi Jonathan Magonet, who gave advice about Jewish commentators.

Thanks are due to the following for permission to reproduce copyright material:

The Archbishop's Council for the Church of England for extracts from *Common Worship: Services and Prayers for the Church of England* (Church House Publishing 2000) and *Common Worship: Pastoral Services* (Church House Publishing 2000) © The Archbishop's Council 2000, reproduced by permission; also for the Preface for Creation, Harvest, from *Patterns for Worship* (Church House Publishing 1995) © The International Commission on English in the Liturgy 1970, reproduced by permission of the publishers; Cambridge University Press for extracts from *The Book of Common Prayer*, the rights in which are vested in the Crown, reproduced by permission of the Crown's Patentee, Cambridge University Press; The Church of the Province of Southern Africa for an extract from *An Anglican Prayer Book* © 1989 The Provincial Trustees of the Church of the Province of Southern Africa; Broughton Books for material from *A Prayer Book for Australia* © 1995 The Anglican Church of Australia Trust Corporation; The Church of the Province of New Zealand for quotations from *A New Zealand Prayer Book – He Karakia Mihinare o Aotearoa* © 1989 and 1997 The Provincial Secretary, The Church of the Province of New Zealand; The Anglican Church of Kenya for a quotation from *A Kenyan Liturgy for Holy Communion* (1989); The Grail (England) for quotations from *The Psalms – The Grail Translation – inclusive language version* © The Grail 1993, used by permission of The Grail (England) and GIA; A. P. Watt & Co. Ltd for extracts from *The Divine Office* © 1974 the hierarchies of Australia, England and Wales, Ireland;

International Commission on English in the Liturgy for excerpts from the English translation of *Rite of Holy Week* © 1972 International Committee on English in the Liturgy, Inc (ICEL); excerpts from the English translation of *The Roman Missal* © 1973, ICEL; excerpts from the English Translation of *Order of*

Christian Funerals © 1985 ICEL, all rights reserved; excerpts from the English translation of *Pastoral Care of the Sick* © 1982, ICEL;

Methodist Publishing House for extracts from *The Methodist Worship Book* © 1999 Trustees for Methodist Church Purposes, and a quotation from *Beyond Tomorrow* by Neville Ward © 1981 Epworth Press. All used by permission of Methodist Publishing House;

Iona Community for extracts from 'The Morning Service' from *The Iona Abbey Worship Book* (2001) and the 'Litany of Violence' from *The Pattern of Our Days* (1996), both © Wild Goose Publications, the Iona Community, Glasgow; The Wild Goose Resource Group for an extract from 'Do not keep silent, O God' from *Psalms of Patience, Protest and Praise* (Wild Goose Publications 1993), words by John Bell © 1993 WGRG, Iona Community, Glasgow; Jane A. Keene for an extract from *A Winter's Song: A Liturgy for Women Seeking Healing from Sexual Abuse in Childhood* (New York: © 1991 The Pilgrim Press); SPCK for extracts from 'All Desires Known' © Janet Morley 1992, and *Christ the Sacramental Word* edited by David Brown and Ann Loades © the editors and contributors 1966 for a quotation from Rowan Williams, and SPCK and Dr Mary Grey for an extract from *Redeeming the Dream* © Mary Grey 1989;

The Society of St Francis for material from *Celebrating Common Prayer* (Mowbray) © The Society of Saint Francis 1992, used with permission.

The Corrymeela Community for a quotation from *Celebrating Together* © Corrymeela Press (1987); Resource Publications Inc. for material from *Celebrating the Earth* by Scott Mc Carthy © 1991 Resource Publications, Inc. All rights reserved. Reprinted with permission;

The United Synagogue for extracts from *The Authorised Daily Prayer Book* © 1998; The Reform Synagogues of Great Britain for extracts from *Forms of Prayer for Jewish Worship* Vol. 1 (*Daily and Sabbath Prayer Book*) London 1977 and Vol. 3 (*Prayers for the High Holydays*) London 1985, both volumes © Reform Synagogues of Great Britain;

Dr Sebastian Brock for translations from Syriac; Peter Sherwood for his translation of the Hungarian Vég Mihály's metrical psalm for this book; Society of Jesus (British Province) for a quotation from 'Nondum' by Gerard Manley Hopkins;

The Orion Publishing Group Ltd for a quotation from R. S. Thomas' poem 'Kneeling' from *Collected Poems 1945–1990* (Phoenix 1995): James Carney for his translation of the poem 'A Chrinoc', from *Mediaeval Irish Lyrics* (Dolmen Press 1985) © James Carney, by permission of Colin Smythe Ltd;

Faber and Faber Ltd for a quotation from David Jones' *Epoch and Artist* © David Jones 1959; St Paul's Publishing for a translation of Hildegard of Bingen in the author's book *The Heart of Love* © St Paul Publications UK 1991; Random House Group for an extract from *Autobiography* by Eric Gill published by Jonathan Cape, used by permission of The Random House Group Limited; Alan Bowness for a quotation from *Some Statements by Barbara Hepworth* © Alan Bowness, Hepworth

Estate 1977; Harper Collins Publishers Ltd for extracts from *Prayers for Pilgrims* ©
Sheila Cassidy 1980;
   Golgonooza Press for extracts from Philip Sherrard's *The Sacred in Life and Art*
(© Philip Sherrard 1990) and *Human Image: World Image* (© Philip Sherrard
1992), also from *Cecil Collins – The Vision of the Fool* (© Elizabeth Collins 1994);
St Vladimir's Seminary Press for extracts from *The Eucharist* by A. Schmemann
(© 1987 St Vladimir's Seminary Press) and *The Aesthetic Face of Being* by V.
Bychkov (© 1993 St Vladimir's Seminary Press); Indiana University Press for an
extract from Herbert Levine's *Sing Unto God a New Song* (© 1995 Herbert J.
Levine); The Pastoral Press for an extract from Lawrence Hoffman's *The Art of
Public Prayer* (© 1988 The Pastoral Press); SCM Press for material from *The Poet,
The Warrior, The Prophet* by Rubem Alves (© Rubem A. Alves 1990); Penguin
Books Ltd for a quotation from *The Prayers and Meditations of Saint Anselm* (©
Benedicta Ward 1973); The Liturgical Press for a quotation from John F.
Craghan's *Psalms for all Seasons* (© 1993 The Order of St Benedict Inc.); Orbis
Books for an extract from Pablo Galdámez' *Faith of a People* (© 1986
Orbis Books);
   Darton, Longman & Todd for material from *N. F. S. Grundtvig* by A. M. Allchin
(© Aarhus University Press); and *To Heaven with Scribes and Pharisees* (© 1975
Lionel Blue); Heythrop College for a quotation from *The Way* vol. 33. 2 (1991,
98 'Boundary Dwellers' by Hannah Ward, reproduced by kind permission of the
Editors, Heythrop College, London; Doubleday Dell Publishing for a quotation
from *Return of the Prodigal Son* by Henri Nouwen (DLT 1994);
   Taizé Community for material from *Never a Stranger* by Br. Emile and *Chantes de
Taizé* © Ateliers et Presses de Taizé 71250 Taizé Community, France; Sheed &
Ward for a quotation from *The Cosmic Covenant* by Robert Murray © Robert
Murray 1992; Sisters of the Love of God for quotations from *Facing Depression* by
Gonville ffrench-Beytagh, SLG Press 1978 © Sisters of the Love of God; Fr
Francis Acharya and Kurisumala Ashram for material from *Prayer with the Harp of
the Spirit* Vol 1 (1983); Abhishiktānanda Society for quotations from *Saccidānanda*
by Abhishiktānanda (Delhi 1984) © Abhishiktānanda Society.
   Every attempt has been made to trace the owners of copyright and any
omissions will be corrected in any further edition. Translations from the Scriptures and other unattributed versions including liturgical texts and hymns are the
work and copyright of the author.

Sources

Numbering of psalms

This book follows the Hebrew numbering of the psalms rather than that of the Greek Septuagint or Latin Vulgate commonly used in Roman Catholic and Orthodox churches. The numbering of verses follows the New Revised Standard Version, as Hebrew numbering includes the title and Psalters vary in their division of the text.

Jewish sources

ADPB   *Authorised Daily Prayer Book* (London 1998)
BT   *Babylonian Talmud* ed. I. Epstein (London 1935–52)
FPJW   *Forms of Prayer for Jewish Worship* (London vol. 1 1977; vol. 2 1921; vol. 3 1985)

Greek Orthodox sources

Megas Ieros Synekdemos tou Orthodoxou Christianou (Phos, Athens 1984)
Ayiasmatarion To Mega (Saliveros, Athens)

Oriental sources

Syrian Orthodox Liturgy of St James (New Jersey 1967)
Ma'de'dono (Book of Church Festivals, New Jersey 1984)
The Sacrament of Holy Baptism (New Jersey 1974)
Burial Rites of the Syrian Orthodox Church (New Jersey 1974)
The Liturgy of St James as presently used, Phillip Tovey (Grove Books 1998)
Prayer with the Harp of the Spirit (Kurisumala Ashram 1983–86)
Rituale Armenorum ed. F. C. Conybeare & A. J. Maclean (Oxford 1905)
Coptic Offices ed. R. M. Woolley (London 1930)
Coptic Morning Service ed. John Marquis of Bute (London 1882)
Ethiopic Liturgy ed. S. A. B. Mercer (London 1915)

Roman Catholic sources (with *Grail Psalter* rev. 1995)
Roman Missal (1973)
Roman Lectionary (1981)
Roman Divine Office (1974)
Pastoral Care of the Sick (1982)
Order of Christian Funerals (1989)

Patristic sources

CCL	*Corpus Christianorum – Series Latina*
PG	*Patrologia Graeca*
PL	*Patrologia Latina*
SC	*Sources Chrétiennes*
CSCO (S)	*Corpus Scriptorum Christianorum Orientalium – Scriptores Syri*

Anglican and Episcopal sources
Book of Common Prayer (England 1662)
Common Worship (England 2000)
Celebrating Common Prayer (England 1992)
The Daily Office (Society of St Francis, Europe rev. 1992)
Book of Common Prayer (USA 1979)
Book of Alternative Services (Canada 1985)
Liturgy for Holy Communion (Kenya 1989)
An Anglican Prayer Book (South Africa 1989)
A New Zealand Prayer Book (1989, 1997)
A Prayer Book for Australia (1996)
Y Llyfr Gweddi Gyffredin (Wales 1984)

Reformed sources
The Book of Common Order (Church of Scotland 1994)
The Methodist Worship Book (Great Britain 1999)

Ecumenical sources
The Book of Worship (Church of North India 1995)
Celebrating Together (Corrymeela, Belfast 1987)
The Pattern of Our Days (Iona Community 1996)
Psalms of Patience, Protest and Praise (Iona Community 1993)
The Iona Abbey Worship Book (Iona Community 2001)
Church Services for the Farming Year (Royal Agricultural Society of England 1989)

Notes

Chapter 1: *On the Edge of Glory*

1. Hannah Ward, 'Boundary Dwellers', *The Way* (London 1991) vol. 33.2, 98.
2. *Pedeir Keinc y Mabinogi* ed. Ifor Williams (Cardiff 1964): Branwen Uerch Lyr, 46–7.
3. Arnold Van Gennep, *The Rites of Passage* tr. M. B. Vizedom and G. L. Caffee (London 1960).
4. Victor Turner, *The Ritual Process* (London 1969), 145.
5. *The Midrash on Psalms* ed. W. G. Braude (New Haven 1959) vol. 2, 243.
6. John Chrysostom, *Eis ton PM Psalmon*, PG 55.427.
7. E. C. Kingsbury, *The Prophets and the Council of Yahweh* JBL **83** (1964) 279–86.
8. Tertullian, *De Oratione* 3.3, CCL 1.259.
9. Cecil Collins, *The Vision of the Fool and other writings* ed. B. Keeble (Ipswich 1994), 'The Theatre of the Soul' (1981), 119–20.
10. Jacob Vellian, *Syro–Malabar Liturgy 1* (East Syrian Raza). (Kottayam, Kerala c. 1989) 58–9.
11. Robert Taft, *The Great Entrance*. Orientalia Christiana Analecta 200 (Rome, Pontifical Institute of Oriental Studies 1975) 84.
12. Bryan D. Spinks, *The Sanctus in the Eucharistic Prayer* (Cambridge 1991) 120–1.
13. *Ortha nan Gaidheal* ed. Alexander Carmichael (Edinburgh 1928) vol. 1, 133; Urdu song 'Yisu ne Kaha', 'Jesus the Lord said, I am the Bread'; Rev. 3.8, 20; 10.7, *cf.* John 10.7–9.
14. Geoffrey Rowell, *The Liturgy of Christian Burial* (London 1977) 57–60. F. S. Paxton, *Christianizing Death* (Ithaca 1990) 39–42; *cf. Liber Sacramentorum Gellonensis*, CCL 159.463.
15. Sigmund Mowinckel, *The Psalms in Israel's Worship* (Oxford 1967) vol. 1, 11, 120, 123, 131; Prudentius, *Cathemerinon* 10.161–72, CCL 126.59.
16. *Midrash Leqach Tob* on Numbers 24.17.
17. Epiphanius, *Tōi hagiōi kai megalōi Sabbatōi*, PG 43.459. *cf.* Sozomenos, *Ekklesiastikē Historia* 7.19, PG 67.1478–9.
18. J. Firmicus Maternus, *De Errore Profanarum Religionum* 25, PL 12.1035–6;

Ernst Kähler, *Studien zum Te Deum und zur Geschichte des 24. Psalms in der alten Kirche. Veröffentlichungen der Evangelischen Gesellschaft für Liturgieforschung* (Göttingen 1958) Heft 5. 65 ff.

19. O. H. E. Burmeister, *La Lectionnaire de la Semaine Sainte. Patrologia Orientalis* 25(2) (Paris 1939) 448; *The Book of Cerne* ed. A. B. Kuypers (Cambridge 1902) Prayer 19. 15–16, 116, 253–4; A. J. MacGregor, *Fire and Light in the Western Triduum* (Collegeville 1992) 278.

20. Karl Young, 'The Harrowing of Hell in Liturgical Drama', *Transactions of the Wisconsin Academy of Sciences, Arts and Letters* (Madison 1910) vol. 16, part 2, 889–947; *Benedictine Ordinal of the Nuns of Barking* MS 169, Library of University College, Oxford; William Langland, *Piers the Plowman* (Text B) ch. 18; *Everyman and Mediaeval Miracle Plays* ed A. C. Cawley (London 1956) 163–5 'The Chester Pageant'.

21. *Manuale Ambrosianum* ed. M. Magistretti (Milan 1904) vol. 2, 485.

22. *Taking up the Timbrel* ed. Sylvia Rothschild and Sybil Sheridan (London 2000) 61–66.

23. ibid. 14–15, 90–91.

24. Jonathan Magonet, *A Rabbi Reads the Psalms* (London 1994) 119–27.

25. David Scott, *An Anglo-Saxon Passion* (London 1999) xxiii–xxiv.

Chapter 2: Second Sight

1. N. I. Ndiokwere, *Prophecy and Revolution* (London 1981) 106–11.

2. Christopher Moody, *Eccentric Ministry* (London 1992) 117.

3. L. A. Hoffman, *The Art of Public Prayer* (Washington DC 1988) 192–3.

4. R. J. Tournay, *Seeing and Hearing God with the Psalms* (Sheffield 1991) 76–86.

5. Dag Hammarskjöld, *Markings* tr. W. H. Auden and Leif Sjoberg (London 1964) 104.

6. Gregory of Nyssa, *Theoria eis ton tou Mouseös Bion* 2.252, SC 1, 280.

7. Lancelot Andrewes, *Preces Privatae Quotidianae Graece et Latine* (London 1848) Part 2, *Preces Matutinae* 259.

8. *An Interrupted Life – The Diaries of Etty Hillesum* (1941–3) ed. J. G. Gaarlandt tr. Arno Pomerans (New York 1983) 173.

9. Robin Green, *Only Connect* (London 1987) 54–6.

10. H. W. Robinson, *Prophetic Symbolism. Old Testament Essays* 1927. 9–10.

11. Raphael Patai, *Man and Temple in Ancient Jewish Myth and Ritual* (London 1947) 131–2.

12. Alexander Schmemann, *The Eucharist* (New York 1988) 34–40.

13. Raphael Patai, *op. cit.* 108; B. T. Sukkah 51b, 244.

14. BT Menahoth 28b, 184.

15. Sister Vandana, *Waters of Fire* (Bangalore 1989) 32.

16. Euripides, *Ion* 5.223–5; Pindar, *Pythia* 4.121–2; Raphael Patai, *op.cit.* 85.

17. Cyril of Jerusalem, *Mystagogical Catecheses* 2.4, PG 33.1080.

18. *Liber Graduum 12. Patrologia Syriaca 3* (1926) ed. M. Kmosko 285 ff. tr. S. P. Brock, *The Syrian Fathers on Prayer and the Spiritual Life* (Kalamazoo 1987) 48.

19. Ephrem, *Hymns of Faith* 81, 83. CSCO (S) 73.

20. Philip Sherrard, *The Sacred in Life and Art* (Ipswich 1990) 17.

21. *Irder byd* Gwaith Tudur Aled, ed. T. Gwyn Jones (Cardiff 1926) vol 2, 524–5.

22. Jyoti Sahi, *Meditations on Symbols of St John's Gospel* (Pune 1978).

23. Hippolytus, *Sermo in Sancta Theophania*, PG 10.858–9.

Chapter 3: *The Call of Love*

1. Margaret Guenther, *Holy Listening* (London 1992) 45.

2. 'A Chrínoc, Cubaid do Cheol' by Mael Ísu Ó Brolcháin. tr. James Carney. *Mediaeval Irish Lyrics* (Mountrath 1985) 74–9.

3. F. Berk (ed.), *The Jewish Dance* (New York 1960) 25, *cf.* BT Sukkah 52b; Mishnah: Sukkah 51b.

4. Ps. 110.1; Num. 24.3; 2 Sam. 23.1; 2 Kings 22.19; Isa. 30.1; 49.18; Jer. 8.3; Ezek. 37.14; Mal. 1. 1.2.

5. Robert Taft, *The Liturgy of the Hours in East and West* (Collegeville 1986) 63, 122, 284.

6. Nicholas Cabasilas, *A Commentary on the Divine Liturgy* tr. J. M. Hussey and P. A. McNutty (London 1960) 58.

7. Terence Bailey (ed.), *The Fleury Play of Herod.* Pontifical Institute of Mediaeval Studies (Toronto 1965) 49.

8. BT Sukkah 51b.243.

9. Robert Murray, *The Cosmic Covenant* (London 1992) 79–80.

10. Pablo Galdámez, *The Faith of a People* tr. R. Barr (London 1986) 61.

11. *Tractate Sanhedrin* ed. H. Freedman (London 1935) vol. 2 (11.98a) 664.

12. Antonio Reiser and P. G. Schoenborn, *Sehnsucht nach dem Fest der Freien Menschen* (Wuppertal 1982) 38–9.

13. Janet Morley, *All Desires Known* (London 1992) 58–9.

14. *Church Services for the Farming Year* (Royal Agricultural Society of England 1989) Lammas Service 4:4.

15. S. R. Hirsch (ed), *The Psalms* (Jerusalem 1978) part 2. 105–6.

16. *cf.* Pss. 12.5; 126.6; 37.11, 17–19: 112.4; 24.3–4; 37.37.

17. Ambrose, *De Sacramentis* 3.1; L. Duchesne, *Christian Worship* (London 1904) 326; *The Stowe Missal* ed. G. F. Warner (Woodbridge 1989) Vol 2.32.

18. Eph. 1.1, 4; Ps. 92.13–14; John 15.5; Pss. 119.1–5, 117; 106.4; 138.8.

19. Philo, *Peri Biou Theoretikou* ed. F. C. Conybeare (Oxford 1895) 127–35.

20. John Chrysostom, *Eis ton MA' Psalmon*, PG 55.163.

21. John Eaton, 'Music's Place in Worship – A Contribution from the Psalms' *Oudtestamentische Studien* **23** (1983) 100.

22. Christoph Wetzel, *Die Psalmen in Bachs Kantaten – 'Bach als Ausleger der Bibel'* ed. Martin Petzoldt (Berlin 1985) 133–4.

23. Kodály's text of Psalmus Hungaricus comes from the metrical version of the sixteenth-century poet Vég Mihály tr. for this book by Peter Sherwood (London University).

Chapter 4: *Searching for Faith*

1. Bernard of Clairvaux, *De Diligendo Deo* 7.22, PL 182.987.
2. Simone Weil, *Attente de Dieu* (Paris 1967) 192–3.
3. Gregory the Great, *Homiliae in Evangelia* 2.29, PL 76.1219.
4. John Donne, *Sermons on the Psalms and the Gospels* ed. E. M. Simpson (Berkeley 1963), Sermon on Psalm 63.7, 107.
5. *The Prayers and Meditations of St Anselm* ed. Benedicta Ward (London 1973) 97–8.
6. *Taking up the Timbrel* ed. Sylvia Rothschild and Sybil Sheridan (London 2000) 9.
7. *Mystical Treatises by Isaac of Nineveh* tr. A. J. Wensinck (Amsterdam 1923) 328, quoted in A. M. Allchin; *Heart of Compassion* (London 1973) 46.
8. Ignatius, *Epistole Magnesieusin* 8.
9. Søren Kierkegaard, *Purity of Heart is to Will One Thing* tr. Douglas Steere (London 1961) 43.
10. *Institutio Generalis Missalis Romani* (1969, rev. 1973) para. 23.
11. Thomas R. Kelly, 'The Gathered Meeting' in *The Friend* (Philadelphia 1940–1) vol. 114, 201–5.
12. Herbert J. Levine, *Sing Unto God a New Song* (Bloomington 1995) 204–12.
13. Mary Grey, *Redeeming the Dream* (London 1989) 68.
14. *The Book of Margery Kempe* ed. Sanford Brown Meech (London 1940) Bk 1.20.48.
15. Guerric of Igny, *Sermones 1: In Nativitate Domini*, SC 166, 164.
16. F. E. Warren, *The Liturgy and Ritual of the Celtic Church* (2nd ed. Woodbridge 1987) 170 (*Book of Dimma*); *The Use of Salisbury – The Ordinary of the Mass* ed. Nick Sandon (2nd ed. Newton Abbot 1990) 6; G. S. M. Walker, *Sancti Columbani Opera* (Dublin 1957) 128–33; Paul Bradshaw, *Daily Prayer in the Early Church* (London 1981) 119–20.
17. Graham Woolfenden, *Daily Prayer in Christian Spain* (London 2000) 48–53.
18. Ephrem, *Hymns on the Nativity* 1.61. CSCO(S) 82. Tr. S. P. Brock. *The Luminous Eye* (Kalamazoo 1992) 140.
19. Christopher Moody. *Eccentric Ministry* (London 1992) 87.
20. Thomas Traherne, *Centuries of Meditation* 4.55.
21. S. R. Hirsch (ed.), *The Psalms* (Jerusalem 1978) part 1.179.
22. H. S. Davies, 'Mistah Kurtz – He Dead', in Allen Tate (ed.) *T. S. Eliot – The Man, His Work* (1967).
23. J. Neil Alexander, *Waiting for the Coming* (Washington DC 1993) 3.
24. Jonathan Magonet, *A Rabbi Reads the Psalms* (London 1994) 81–2.
25. J. Neil Alexander, *op. cit.* 93–5.
26. S. R. Hirsch (ed.), *op. cit.* part 2.6–8.

Chapter 5: *Love Rediscovered*

1. Eric Gill, *Autobiography* (London 1940) 247.
2. Julian of Norwich, *A Revelation of Love* ed. M. Glascoe (Exeter 1986) ch. 78, 94.
3. S. R. Hirsch (ed), *The Psalms* (Jerusalem 1978) part 1. 362.
4. Martin Buber, *Ich und Du* (Köln 1966) 18, 73.
5. Pavel Florensky, *Stolp i utverzhdenie istiny (The Pillar and Foundation of Truth)* (Moscow 1914) 438–9, quoted in Robert Slesinski, *Pavel Florensky, A Metaphysics of Love* (New York 1984) 221–2. John Chrysostom, *Homilia B eis ten pros Thessalonikeis Ep. A.* PG 62.406.
6. Basil, *Epistle* 207, PG 32.763
7. *Gelasian Sacramentary* 1,38 cf. *Rituale Armenorum* 204.
8. Maimonides, *Mishneh Torah-Laws of Repentance* 1.1.
9. Monford Harris, *Exodus and Exile* (Minneapolis 1992) 58.
10. *Codex Latinus Monacensis* 935 der Bayerischen Staatsbibliothek. Oratio 29. Tr. B. L. Pickett, *The Heart of Love* (Slough 1991) 53.
11. Karen Pusey, *Jewish Proselyte Baptism* (Swansea 1993) 64–5.
12. Chasidic, quoted in FPJW 3: *Study Anthology* 766.
13. Charles Williams, 'The Redeemed City', *Dublin Review* (Oct 1941).
14. Sebastian Brock, *The Luminous Eye* (Kalamazoo 1992) 85–97, including the translations of Ephrem quoted here.
15. 'Joseph the Visionary', Mingana syr 564 fol 178b-181b (1931) tr. Sebastian Brock, *The Syriac Fathers on Prayer and the Spiritual Life* (Kalamazoo 1987) 355–7.
16. Philip Sherrard, *The Sacred in Life and Art* (Ipswich 1990) 63.
17. Sebastian Brock, *The Holy Spirit in the Syrian Baptismal Tradition* (Poona 1998) 161, quoting Ephrem, *De Virq* 7 cf. CSCO(S) 94.
18. B. L. Pickett, *The Heart of Love* (Slough 1991) 66, quoting Hildegard, *Symphonia Armoniae Celestium Revelationum* ed. Pudentia Barth (Salzburg 1969) no. 15.
19. Julian of Norwich, *op.cit.* ch. 38, 39.
20. Martin Buber, *Die Legende des Baal-Schem* (Frankfurt a M 1918), *Shiflut* 35–7.
21. Walter Brueggemann, *The Message of the Psalms* (Minneapolis 1984) 101.
22. David Holeton, 'Penance and the Eucharist' in *Revising the Eucharist* Alcuin/Grow Lit Study **27** (Nottingham 1994) 39–40. B. L. Pickett, *Text for Peace.*
23. *The Book of Margery Kempe* ed. Sanford Brown Meech (London 1939) Book 2, 10. 251.
24. Charles Williams, *The Descent of the Dove* (London 1939) 2. 28; *The Forgiveness of Sins* (London 1942) ch. 5; 'The Redeemed City' *Dublin Review* (Oct 1941).
25. Henri Nouwen, *The Return of the Prodigal Son* (New York 1992) 119.

Chapter 6: *The Dew of the Dawn*

1. H. Birkeland, *Die Feinde des Individuums in der israelitischer Psalmenliteratur* (Oslo 1933). J. H. Eaton, *Kingship and the Psalms* (2nd ed. Sheffield 1986) 20–6.

2. Abhishiktānanda, *Saccidānānda – A Christian Approach to Advaitic Experience* (Delhi rev. 1984) 107–8.

3. F. Neugebauer, 'Die Davidssohnfrage und der Menschenssohn' *NTS* 21 (1974–5) 81–92.

4. Janet Morley, *All Desires Known* (London 1992) xi–xii.

5. James Nelson, *The Intimate Connection* (London 1992) 45–6.

6. Janet Morley, *ibid*.

7. Walter Brueggemann, *Israel's Praise* (Philadelphia 1988) 70.

8. J. M. Spencer (ed.), 'The Worshipping Church in Africa. Black Sacred Music'; *A Journal of Theomusicology* 7 (2) (Duke University 1993) 48; Nwaka Chris Egbulem, *The Power of Africentric Celebrations* (New York 1996) 95–6; 136–7.

9. R. Tournay, *Seeing and Hearing God in the Psalms* (Sheffield 1991) 223–4.

10. Cyril of Jerusalem, *Mystagogical Catecheses* 2.3; 3.1.

11. E. C. Whitaker, *Documents of the Baptismal Liturgy* (2nd ed. London 1970) 12.

12. Sebastian P. Brock, 'Spirituality in the Syriac Tradition', *Mōrān 'Eth'ō* Series 2 (Kottayam 1989) 50–51.

13. Tertullian, *De Baptismo* 7, CCL 1. 282.

14. Ambrose, *De Mysteriis* 6.30 ed. B. Botte (Paris 1905) 117 *cf*. PL16.415.

15. C. Wordsworth, *Ceremonies and Processions of the Cathedral Church of Salisbury* (Cambridge 1901) 106.

16. J. F. Craghan, *Psalms for All Seasons* (Collegeville 1993) 78.

17. Sebastian Brock, *The Holy Spirit in the Syrian Baptismal Tradition* (Pune 1998) 157–8.

18. David Taylor, 'The Great Psalm Commentary of Daniel of Salah' in *The Harp*. SEERI (Kottayam 1998–9) vols 11–12, 41.

19. A. Schmemann, *The World as Sacrament* (London 1966) 128–9.

20. Augustine, *Confessiones* 9.12, PL 32.776.

21. Gerard Manley Hopkins; 'God's Grandeur'.

22. Gregory the Great, *Homilia in Evangelia* 1. Hom 12, PL 76.1120.

23. J. H. Eaton, 'Music's Place in Worship: A Contribution from the Psalms' *Oudtestamentische Studiën* 23 (1983) 102.

24. Jonathan Magonet, *A Rabbi Reads the Psalms* (London 1994) 49–50.

25. Rabbi Elie Munck, *The World of Prayer* (New York 1962–3) vol. 2, 8.

Chapter 7: *Descent into Darkness*

1. A. J. MacGregor, *Fire and Light in the Western Triduum* (Collegeville 1992) 131–2.

2. Gonville ffrench-Beytagh, *Facing Depression* (Fairacres, Oxford 1978) 2.

3. Jane A. Keene, *A Winter's Song* (Cleveland 1991) 4–6.

4. Sheila Cassidy, *Prayer for Pilgrims* (London 1980) 134.

5. Dietrich Bonhoeffer, *The Psalms – Prayer Book of the Bible* (Fairacres, Oxford 1982) 17.

6. André Néher, *The Exile of the Word – From the Silence of the Bible to the Silence of Auschwitz* tr. David Maisel (Philadelphia 1981) 68–9.

7. Avot 4.23; Berachot 3.1

8. André Néher, *op.cit.* 86.

9. Gregory of Nyssa, *Theoria eis ton tou Mouseos Biou* 2.163–4, SC 1.210, 212.

10. Gonville ffrench-Beytagh, *op. cit.* 6.

11. W. G. Braude, *The Midrash on Psalms* (New Haven 1959) vol. 2, 334.

12. Shapiro of Warsaw, 'Sermon of March 14, 1942' quoted in *The Literature of Destruction - Jewish Responses to Catastrophe* ed. David Roskies (Philadelphia 1989) 508.

13. Sheila Cassidy, *op. cit.* 136

14. Dietrich Bonhoeffer, *op.cit.* 16–17.

15. W. G. Henderson, *Processionale ad usum Ecclesiae Sarum* (Leeds 1882) 8; William Langland, *Piers the Ploughman* tr. J. F. Goodridge (London 1966) Appendix A from the C text 258; J. Foster, *The Church of the T'ang Dynasty* (London 1939) 137.

16. Catherine Pickstock, *After Writing* (Oxford 1998) 154–5.

17. Isa. 13.8; Jer. 22.23, 41, 48; 49.22; 50.43; Mic. 4.9; Isa. 21.3; 26.17; cf. Isa. 66.9.

18. Gonville ffrench-Beytagh, *Out of the Depths* (Fairacres, Oxford 1990) 19.

19. Margaret Guenther, *Holy Listening* (London 1992) 87.

20. Pavel Florensky, *Bogoslovskie Trudy* vol. 17 (Moscow 1977) 87–248, tr. Victor Bychkov, *The Aesthetic Face of Being* (Crestwood 1993) 64–5.

21. Hildegard, *Liber Divinorum Operum Visio* 4.12, 29, PL 197.812, 826.

22. Abhishiktānanda, *Saccidānanda – A Christian Approach to Advaitic Experience* (Delhi, rev. 1984) 64.

23. T. S. Eliot, Choruses from 'The Rock'.

24. Herbert J. Levine, *Sing Unto God A New Song* (Bloomington 1995) 176.

Chapter 8: *The Lord of the Dance*

1. Canaan Sodindo Banana, *Come and Share* (Gweru, Zimbabwe 1991) 25.

2. A. de Buck, 'La Fleur au front du grand-prêtre,' *OTS* 9 (1951) 18–29.

3. J. H. Eaton: *Kingship and the Psalms* (Sheffield 1986) 179.

4. Aubrey Johnson, *Sacral Kingship in Ancient Israel* (Cardiff 1967) 125.

5. Walter Brueggemann, *Israel's Praise* (Philadelphia 1988) 139.

6. Cecil Collins, *The Vision of the Fool* ed. Brian Keeble (Ipswich 1994) 74–7; also his works *Christ before the Judge* (1956) and *The Crucifixion* (1952).

7. Cecil Collins, *op. cit.* 73.

8. Br Emile, *Never a Stranger* (Taizé 1991) 16–18.

9. Abhishiktānanda, *Saccidānanda – A Christian Approach to Advaitic Experience* (Delhi, rev. 1984) 144.

10. BT Sukkah; Mishnah: Sukka 3.9; 4.5. Hayim Schauss, *Guide to Jewish Holy Days* (New York 1962) 170ff, *cf.* ADPB 671 ff. and John 7.37–9.

11. BT Sukkah: 51b.244

12. Irenaeus, *Adversus Haereses* 4.20.5. SC 100.640.

13. Ephrem, *Hymns of Faith* 10; *Armenian Hymns* 47. Symeon the New Theologian, *Hymns* 6, 30. Wesley, *Hymns on the Lord's Supper* 89, 116. 137 *cf.* 101, also 'Come, Holy Ghost, all-quickening fire'.

14. Rowan Williams, 'Sacraments of the New Society' in *Christ: The Sacramental Word* ed. David Brown and Ann Loades (London 1996) 89–90.

15. Philip Sherrard, *The Sacred in Life and Art* (Ipswich 1990) 84.

16. Theodoret, *Ekklesiastike Historia* 3.22, PG 82. 1120–1.

17. W. G. Henderson, *Processionale ad usum Ecclesiae Sarum* (Leeds 1882) 95.

18. Herbert J. Levine, *Sing Unto God a New Song* (Bloomington 1995) 166.

19. Herbert J. Levine, *op. cit.* 169, 160.

Chapter 9: *A Taste of Paradise*

1. Francis de Sales, *Treatise on the Love of God* Book 6, ch.9 (Douai 1630) *cf.* tr. H. B. Mackey (Westminster 1942). Most translations omit this passage.

2. Acts 27; 2 Cor. 11.26; James 1.6; 1 Cor. 9.9; James 3.3; Acts 18.3, 16.4; 1 Cor. 15.41, 12.22–24, 9.27; Gal. 5.24.

3. Tertullian, *De cultu feminarum* 2.2.4, CCL 1. 355; Augustine, *De Civitate Dei* 14.16; 21.4, PL 41.424, 711; *Conf.* 10.35, 37, PL 32.803; Luther, *Tischreden* (Weimarer Ausgabe) 2.1818.

4. Lionel Blue, *To Heaven with Scribes and Pharisees* (London 1975) 39.

5. Meinrad Craighead, *The Litany of the Great River* (New York 1991) 12.

6. S. P. Brock, *Holy Spirit in the Syrian Baptismal Tradition* (Pune 1998) 126.

7. Robert Murray, *The Cosmic Covenant* (London 1992) 29–32.

8. Neville Ward, *Beyond Tomorrow* (London 1981) 3–4.

9. Chengannur church (thirteenth century) near Tiruvalla, also some paintings at St Mary's, Kaduthuruthy and Cheryapalli, Kottayam (both sixteenth century), all in Kerala.

10. Dafydd ap Gwilym, *Offeren y Ceiliog Bronfraith a'r Eos.*

11. *Prayer with the Harp of the Spirit* ed. Francis Acharya (Kurisumala Ashram Kerala 1983) vol. 1.95–6.

12. Nativity: Roman sarcophagus *c.* 333; relief from Naxos *c.* 400 (Byzantine Museum, Athens). Orpheus: third-century Roman catacomb of Domitilla; fourth-century relief (Byzantine Museum, Athens).

13. F. E. Brightman, *Liturgies Eastern and Western* (Oxford 1896) 125, 50, 14–16; S. McCarthy, *Celebrating the Earth* (San José 1987) 119–22.

14. PL 85, part 1.613 (Hispanic Rite *cf.* Holy Communion Rite of the Spanish Reformed Episcopal Church 1894); Cyril of Jerusalem, *Mystagogical Catecheses* 5.20, PG 33.1124; Jerome, *Comment in Es* 2 c5.20; *Horologion of St Sabbas the Sanctified*; Brightman *op. cit.* 25, 63, 450 (Armenian and Syrian rites); F. E. Warren, *The Liturgy and Rites of the Celtic Church* (Woodbridge

2nd ed. 1987) 192, 243, 267 (Antiphonary of Bangor and Stowe Missal); *The Book of Common Order of the Church of Scotland* (1994) 139, 171.

15. Rubem Alves, *The Poet, the Warrior, the Prophet* (London 1990) 84–6.
16. Alves, *op.cit.*, 11–12.
17. Archimandrite Vasileios, *Hymn of Entry* (Crestwood NY 1998) 70–74.
18. Archimandrite Vasileios, *op. cit.* 74.
19. Walter Brueggemann, *The Message of the Psalms* (Minneapolis 1984) 134.
20. The Tympanum of the Basilica of St Mary Magdalene, Vézelay, Burgundy.
21. J. Foster, *The Church of the T'ang Dynasty* (London 1939) 157.
22. Philip Sherrard, *Human Image, World Image* (Ipswich 1992) 151–2.
23. Nicholas Uspensky, *Evening Worship in the Orthodox Church* (Crestwood NY 1985) 106–9.
24. Grundtvig, *Sang Verk* vol. 1 no. 145.325 6 *cf.* Grundtvigs *Prædikener* vol. 7.104 quoted in A. M. Allchin, *N.F.S. Grundtvig* (London 1997) 151, 154.

Chapter 10: *A New Song for the Earth*

1. *Wesley's Covenant Service of 1780 – Directions for Renewing our Covenant with God cf.* David Tripp, *The Renewal of the Covenant in the Methodist Tradition* (London 1969) 181.
2. Augustine, *Sermo 272 Ad Infantes de Sacramento*, PL 38.1247.
3. Irenaeus, *Adversus Haereses* 4.17.3, SC 100.612.
4. Nwaka Chris Egbulem, *The Power of Africentric Celebrations* (New York 1996) 55, 151.
5. Charles Williams, 'The Redeemed City' *Dublin Review* (October 1941) quoted in Charles Williams, *Essential Writings in Spirituality and Theology* ed. Charles Hefling (Boston 1993) 157, 153.
6. Charles Williams took this quotation from the Fourth Lateran Council.
7. George Herbert, 'Providence'.
8. Olivier Clément, 'L'Homme dans le Monde', *Verbum Caro* vol. 12. 45 (1958) 11–12.
9. David Jones, 'Art and Sacrament' (1955) in *Epoch and Artist* ed. Harman Grisewood (London 1959) 166–7.
10. Schlomo Yitzchaki (Rashi): Midrash Psalms 4.11; S. R. Hirsch (ed.), *The Psalms* (Jerusalem 1978) part 1. 23 *cf.* Isa. 49.22; 62.10.
11. *The Life of Blessed Henry Suso* tr. T. F. Knox (London 1913) 11.32.
12. *Patterns for Worship* (1995) 128 based on the Roman Preface for Sundays in Ordinary Time V; *Common Worship* Eucharistic Prayer G.
13. Pierre Teilhard de Chardin, *Hymne de l'Universe* (Paris 1961), 'L'Offrande' 21–2.
14. *Some Statements about Barbara Hepworth* ed. A. Bowness (St Ives 1977) 1.
15. S. R. Hirsch (ed.) *op. cit.*, Book 3.177–9.
16. Abhishiktānanda, *Saccidānanda – A Christian Approach to Advaitic Experience* (Delhi, rev. 1984) 60.
17. BT Berakoth 4b.

18. Gregory the Great, *Homiliae in Evangelia* 1.11.4, PL 76.1116.
19. Richard Hooker, *Laws of Ecclesiastical Polity*. Book 5:56.5.
20. R. Su-Min, *La caverne des trésors* chs 23, 49, CSCO (S) 207. Ephrem, *Nisibene Hymns* 39.7, CSCO (S) 102.24–5.
21. Rosemary Cramp, 'Nature Redeemed' in *The Sense of the Sacramental* ed. David Brown and Ann Loades (London 1995) 130; Jyoti Sahi, *Holy Ground* (Auckland 1998) 26–30 for discussion of the South Indian crosses of Kaduthuruthy and Velliapalli *cf.* the cross of St Thomas' shrine at Mylapore and the Chinese crosses from Ch'üan-chou-fu and Fang-shan.
22. Sebastian Brock, *Spirituality in the Syriac Tradition* (Kottayam 1989) 78 for this translation of Ephrem, *Armenian Hymns* 49.
23. Alan Griffiths, *We Give You Thanks and Praise* (Norwich 1999) 69 for the Ambrosian preface; Charles Wesley's hymn 'My God, I am thine' (1749); Lionel Muirhead's hymn 'The Church of God a kingdom is' (1899).
24. For birds imitating the shape of the cross see Tertullian, *De Oratione* 29, CCL 1 and Ephrem, *Hymns of Faith* 18.6, CSCO(S) 73; on the Ruthwell Cross see Rosemary Cramp, *op. cit.* 128; the elephants are found at Velliapalli church, Kottayam, Kerala.
25. The Liturgy of Addai and Mari *cf.* F. E. Brightman, *Liturgies, Eastern and Western* (Oxford 1896) 302–3.
26. Basil, *Homilia eis ton proton Psalmon*, PG 29.212–13.
27. Dietrich Bonhoeffer, *Widerstand und Ergebung* ed. E. Bethge (München 1951) 192–3, Letter of 20.5.1944.

A Short Bibliography

Jewish perspectives

Rabbi Samson Raphael Hirsch (ed.); *The Psalms* (Feldheim Publishers, Jerusalem/New York 1978)

Herbert J. Levine, *Sing Unto God a New Song* (Indiana University Press, Bloomington 1995)

Jonathan Magonet, *A Rabbi Reads the Psalms* (SCM, London 1994)

Biblical studies

A. A. Anderson, *Psalms* (2 vols) *The New Century Bible Commentary* (Marshall, Morgan & Scott, London 1972)

Walter Brueggemann, *Israel's Praise* (Fortress Press, Philadelphia 1988)

Walter Brueggemann, *The Message of the Psalms* (Augsburg, Minneapolis 1984)

John H. Eaton, *Kingship and the Psalms* (JSOT Press, 2nd ed. 1986)

John H. Eaton, *The Psalms Come Alive* (Mowbray, London 1984)

John H. Eaton, *The Contemplative Face of Old Testament Wisdom* (SCM, London 1989)

S. E. Gillingham, *The Poems and Psalms of the Hebrew Bible* (OUP, Oxford 1994)

Raymond Jacques Tournay, *Seeing and Hearing God with the Psalms* (JSOT 1991)

Liturgical studies

J. A. Lamb, *The Psalms in Christian Worship* (The Faith Press, London 1962)

Massey H. Shepherd Jr, *The Psalms in Christian Worship* (The Liturgical Press, Collegeville 1976)

André Rose, *Les Psaumes* (Editions P. Lethielleux, Paris 1981)

Robert J. Taft, *The Liturgy of the Hours in East and West* (The Liturgical Press, Collegeville 1986)

Stephen Breck Reid (ed.), *Psalms and Practice* (The Liturgical Press, Collegeville 2001)

Spirituality
D. Bonhoeffer, *The Psalms – Prayer Book of the Bible* (Fairacres, Oxford 1982)
Walter Brueggemann, *Praying the Psalms* (St Mary's Press, Winona Minnesota 1982)
John F. Craghan, *Psalms for All Seasons* (The Liturgical Press, Collegeville 1993)

Index

References to the Psalms

References to the Psalms in the New Testament

		Page			Page
Matthew	5.3–9	44, 185 n. 16	John	12.27	58
	6.9	95		19.28	58
	21.9	9, 131		20.17	133
	21.42	131	Acts	4.11	131
	26.38	58, 107		13.33	89
Mark	12.1–12	93, 131	Romans	10.18	50
	12.35–37	93	1 Cor.	15.20–9	133
	15.34	58, 108	Hebrews	1,1–5	89
Luke	3.21–2	93		2.12	133
	9.18–35	93		5.5–6	89
	11.2	95	1 Peter	2.3	153
	20.41 4	89		2.7	131
	23.46	140–1			